Le Bizarre and *Le Décousu* in the Novels and Theoretical Works of Denis Diderot

How the Idea of Marginality Originated in Eighteenth-Century France

LE BIZARRE AND *LE DÉCOUSU* IN THE NOVELS AND THEORETICAL WORKS OF DENIS DIDEROT

How the Idea of Marginality Originated in Eighteenth-Century France

Barbara Lise Abrams

With a Preface by
Jennifer Vanderheyden

The Edwin Mellen Press
Lewiston•Queenston•Lampeter

Library of Congress Cataloging-in-Publication Data

Abrams, Barbara Lise.
  Le bizarre and Le décousu in the novels and theoretical works of Denis Diderot : how the idea of marginality originated in eighteenth-century France / Barbara Lise Abrams ; with a preface by Jennifer Vanderheyden.
    p. cm.
  Includes bibliographical references and index.
  ISBN-13: 978-0-7734-4663-2
  ISBN-10: 0-7734-4663-X
  I. Title.

hors série.

A CIP catalog record for this book is available from the British Library.

Front cover: Greuze, Jean-Baptiste, 1725-1805. *Portrait of Denis Diderot* (1713-1784)
The Pierpont Morgan Library, New York. Gift of Mr. John M. Crawford. 1958.3.

      The Edwin Mellen Press   The Edwin Mellen Press
            Box 450   Box 67
      Lewiston, New York   Queenston, Ontario
       USA 14092-0450   CANADA L0S 1L0

                    The Edwin Mellen Press, Ltd.
                    Lampeter, Ceredigion, Wales
                    UNITED KINGDOM SA48 8LT

              Printed in the United States of America

In loving memory of my father, Arnold Abrams
Scientist, Artist, Man of Letters

Table of Contents

Preface

Many scholars have addressed Jean-Jacques Rousseau's self-appointed representation of the alienated figure in the Age of the Enlightenment, yet few have studied this concept in depth in relation to Denis Diderot. Barbara Abrams does so in this crucial exploration of the marginal in Diderot's works. Although Diderot did not use the exact term, Abrams defines in detail his various connotations of the *marginal*: theoretically, realistically and hypothetically. In addition to her qualifications as a scholar and professor of the French Enlightenment, Abrams' background in the field of domestic violence and protective services for women and children provides her with an added perspective with regard to her discussion of physically imposed marginalization and its psycho-social consequences. Thoroughly grounded in the literature and philosophy of the eighteenth-century French Enlightenment, and trained in both the theoretical and clinical aspects of psychological theory, Abrams is well situated to explore the central theme of this study, that of Diderot's deep and abiding interest in what designates the marginal personality. Abrams' previous research and publications in the field of Eighteenth-Century French literature, especially on the works of Diderot and Rousseau, as well as her research on gender and its representation in eighteenth-century French Literature, are all elaborations, in one manner or another, of the fertile ideas developed in the present work.

Abrams begins her exploration of the marginal in Diderot's works by investigating thoroughly its various definitions and nuances, especially pertaining to the concepts of alienation and *otherness*. The word *marginal* serves as an umbrella for the quite diverse categories that it covers, such as Diderot's use of the terms *génie, bizarre,* and *original*. Here Abrams expounds upon Robert Mauzi's designations of the three types of alienation in Diderot's works to create the categories of forced, self-imposed, and biological marginalization. In the second chapter Abrams makes the salient observation that, although Rousseau and Diderot could each be described as marginal figures, a principal difference resides in the manner by which Rousseau withdrew from society, whereas Diderot remained a "distanced" participant, thereby lending more credibility to his understanding of *the other*. Thus, as Abrams points out, it is logical that Diderot should utilize the dialogic method in *Le Neveu de Rameau* in order to allow this dialectic between the *marginal* (le Neveu) and the philosopher or questioner. And, as Abrams so perceptively remarks, this method disrupts and in a sense alienates the reader as well, mirroring the entire problematic of the marginalized state. A remarkable analysis follows that investigates all aspects of the Nephew's lucid self-marginalization, including Abrams' critical interweaving of current scholars' commentaries (Foucault, Serres, Kristiva, Crocker, among others). In the third chapter Abrams investigates the character of Suzanne in *La Religieuse* in terms of her forced marginalization in the convent, specifically from a psycho-social context. Suzanne's illegitimacy renders her an outsider or marginal figure in her family of origin and her self-alienating personality furthers this isolation in the "family" of the convent. Abrams presents an in-depth analysis of Suzanne's psychodynamic relationships to the various mothers superior, as well as an insightful religious analogy that describes Suzanne's persecution within the convent. In the final chapter Abrams explores Diderot's theoretical writings, both scientific and philosophical, in his quest for the truth, and the manner by which this quest reflects his theories of the numerous connotations of the *marginal*. Abrams' key discovery that Diderot always used the term *décousu* at the same time he used the word *bizarre* sustains and legitimizes her contention that Diderot understood these concepts as a process of "unraveling." This reflects Diderot's materialistic philosophy of everything being in continual movement as well as his scientific propensity for process and methodology.

Finally, Abrams examines the many links between the marginalized genius and the pursuit of truth in a wide range of Diderot's works, and she also reveals important aspects of Diderot's materialist philosophy as it relates to his search for the origins of genius. The definition of genius, a central problematic for Diderot, is shown to be essential to the understanding of the nature of knowledge itself. Abrams is undoubtedly correct in claiming that Diderot's aim, though he expressed it only obliquely, was to demonstrate that it was none other than the genius who comes closest to truth, and this he does while in the process of unraveling. "Enlightened Insanity" is thus a description of the state of the marginalized genius. In choosing this as the thematic of her study, Abrams argues that Diderot described characters as *"bizarre"* and *"décousu"* in order to emphasize this essential connection. One should not underestimate the importance of philological concerns in a study of this nature, and here Abrams, ever alert to the nuance of language and connotation, reminds us of how such concerns can be both entertaining and heuristic.

This particular study fills a gap in the current understanding of Diderot's œuvres because it elaborates a constellation of ideas in the author's work, that in aggregate illuminates not only the great philosophical enterprise of the Age of Enlightenment, but also sheds new light on the background of our present concept of marginality. In a stunning example of "absence is presence," the missing term, "marginality," in Diderot's work, when replaced as a thematic guide in this study, provides the key to understanding a central aspect of the Enlightenment's scientific and literary projects.

As Abrams so skillfully describes, Diderot's characters serve as vehicles in the elaboration of his search for ultimate verity. Abrams directs our attention to Diderot's insight that a genius is a rare being capable of seeing through the hidden unity of a given process and then communicating that unity to others in a creative and cogent manner. The author's claim that the origins of the modern concept of genius are to be found within the French Enlightenment's quest for truth is beautifully and forcefully developed as we are constantly reminded that at a crucial moment in the development of modern thought, specifically in terms of scientific, literary, and political theory, Diderot used every intellectual tool to pursue his important quest. For this reason the present work should hold broad appeal to scholars at all stages of study, in fields well beyond the domains of French literature and French Eighteenth Century Studies.

Jennifer Vanderheyden, Ph.D.
Department of Foreign Languages and Literatures
Marquette University
Milwaukee, Wisconsin

Acknowledgments

I would like to express my gratitude for the valuable guidance of Gita May, and Pierre Force, under whose direction I formed the core of this project. I also wish to acknowledge my colleagues Camille Weiss and Jennifer Vanderheyden and Axa Benjamen for their sustaining encouragement throughout the various stages of my work. For the unconditional love and understanding of my entire family I am deeply grateful. My children Ari and Talia and my mother Naomi have never wavered in their energy and enthusiasm. Finally for my husband David Kudan, whose patience and support sustained me through this project, I find no words to express adequately my appreciation so I will simply say, thank you.

Introduction

This study addresses the topic of *marginality* and Diderot's attempt to define the notion through his many character depictions, speculative definitions and theoretical discussions. Denis Diderot's work is a particularly interesting laboratory for this study in that the concept *marginality* is demonstrated by his characters, and is shaped in many other aspects of his work. The central hypothesis at work in this study is as follows: The concept of *marginality* that emerges from Diderot's work is a direct result of the weaving together of many different types of alienating processes.

This book begins with the etymology of related French and English terms, placing them in their respective historical literary contexts, and then moves beyond the initial scope, using a select range of methodologies to examine the subject from multiple perspectives, drawing from psychoanalytic principles, intertextuality and historical sources. I explore Diderot's initial identification of *marginality*, for his generation and for those to come, as discussed in a selected sampling of his work. Finally, I examine central characters and interpret their actions as expressions of Diderot's attempt to define *marginality*.

Chapter One reveals three distinctive though not mutually exclusive forms of *marginality* and contextualizes the discussion of the chapters that are to follow. This lays the groundwork for the definition of *marginality* developed in this work.

Chapter Two treats the experimental style of writing that reflected the philosophy of the age the Age of Enlightenment Diderot's choice to employ a dialogic style of conversation in *Le Neveu de Rameau,* demonstrates a unique technique specifically designed to affect the readers' consideration of *marginality*. *Le Neveu de Rameau* illustrates the concept of self-appointed distancing or *self-imposed* marginalization. This novel is perhaps the most popular of Diderot's works, and presents a complex interweave of the stylized marginalization of the reader in the dialogue between the two characters: *moi* and *lui*. Throughout the novel we witness the actual interplay of the concept of *self-imposed marginality*. In examining the structure and style of the novel I further explore how Diderot construes a type of alienation between the reader and the text.

Chapter Three provides an in depth look at the epistolary novel in the form of textual analysis, pointing directly to the use of the theme of *marginality*. These newly categorized forms of marginality do not necessarily function in a mutually exclusive manner. In *La Religieuse, forced marginality* and *biologically predetermined marginality* form a specific bond and for that reason serve as a good example for this analysis. Through a detailed discussion of this work, I outline two separate forms of *marginality* and demonstrate how these concepts actually function within the work of Diderot.

Chapter Four explores various philosophical texts of Diderot, in an attempt to reveal the pervasive nature of the theme of *marginality* present in all of his work. This chapter treats several of Diderot's speculative works including *La lettre sur les aveugles* and *Le rêve de d'Alembert.* Here I demonstrate the notion that *marginality* is often experienced in an unraveled state, and by people who live on the edge of their mental boundaries. The notion of *marginality* is an essential component in the emerging definition of genius in the *Encyclopédie*.

Overall, this work is devoted to tracing the evolution of the concept of marginality from its roots in eighteenth-century France, to the highly variegated and complex usage in our own modern discourse, paying special attention to the way in which the philosophical speculation of the period came to inform the ideas that are reflected in the modern usage of the terms *marginal* and marginality. In sum, this book describes some of the various conceptual and timely definitions of *marginality* and examines a part of eighteenth-century French literature that shaped the evolution of the modern usage of the term itself.

As an ensemble, Diderot's work encompasses the linguistic and conceptual range of the notion of *marginality* as an overreaching category that includes far more than the term alienation, for *marginality* encompasses mental, social, and physical alienation. Denis Diderot stands squarely in the midst of this process, and although he never formally employed the French term *marginal* and only indirectly approached a definition of *marginality,* he addressed the problematic in practically all of his works. Indeed, Diderot was systematic in his treatment of a plethora of related terms current in his epoch. My main goal in this study is to present those discussions by demonstrating that as an ensemble Diderot's work in particular addresses and even shapes what have come to be the salient pertinent aspects of our present concept of *marginality*

Chapter One
Tracing the Margins:
Defining Marginality in Context

This chapter defines the notion of *marginality* as it appears in the works of Denis Diderot. First I treat the context and the backdrop of early-modern France by exploring the uses of the word marginality within this context. I survey other words that were used in place of the term marginality, yet that relate directly to its modern day usage. The discussion that outlines the background of the concept of *marginality* also reveals the underlying relationship of the contemporary term *marginal* to French terms employed similarly in eighteenth-century France and as such traces its evolution through the early-modern period. Finally, I present three distinctive forms of marginality which are central to Diderot's exploration of the concept.

The terms *marginality, alienation*, and *the other* continue to evoke interest and stimulate lively debate in regard to their respective interpretations and functions within the Academy. Despite the exciting critical space opened by these concepts, with their popularity they begin to lose their meaning if severed from their particular histories, contexts, and evolutions. The current usage of the term *marginal* derived from the context of early-modern European society, and in pre-revolutionary France.

Throughout the range of Diderot's works including both speculative and creative pieces, one finds an array of interdependent terms that describe aspects of *marginality*. In retrospect it appears that Diderot engaged in the methodical exploration of the concept that today is referred to as *marginality*. His work demonstrates constant attempts to define *marginality*, if not directly, then certainly obliquely.

The term *marginal*, as used today, may apply to an individual, or to groups of individuals, who for various reasons such as construed illegitimacy of birth, mental illness, or gender preferences may be alienated from society and therefore relegated to an existence on the fringes of the notional center of social life. To further complicate the matter, we have come to use the word *marginal* to refer figuratively to that which stands outside the norm. In the broader sense, margins are both physical and metaphorical, and the term may denote the person, process, or even the degree to which a person, activity, or concept is excluded, pushed to the side, rejected, or held in contempt. The very broad usage of the term *marginality* in the twentieth century can be traced to the establishment of the margins of eighteenth-century French society and the psychological parameters set by its intelligentsia and ruling classes. Today the term thus serves as an umbrella for the varying types of movement away from the norm by certain groups or individuals.

Many of Diderot's fictional characters were based on real people, and from his characters one can perceive that society was defined not only in terms of who fit in, but also in terms of those who did not. The characters Diderot created in his fiction provide evidence that he recognized more than one type of *marginal* personality. Other key words used by Diderot that signify *marginality* include *bizarre* and *original.* These terms are presently used to describe what is known as *marginal.*

The term *marginality* unveils the first problematic of this study because it used to define a plethora of subjects. This ambiguity of usage exists because *marginality* is often conflated with a number of other related concepts. The term could also be confusing because it is used retrospectively to address concepts in an age when the word itself was not used in the same context. Older definitions included in the *Oxford Dictionary* as early as 1700 do not reflect this abstract or extended connotation.[1] The French word *marginal* was literally interpreted in the

---

[1] The *Oxford English Dictionary*, for example, states that the word *marginal* is "characterized by the incorporation of habits and values from two divergent cultures and by incomplete assimilation in either," which here is described as other, or "those located on the fringe of consciousness," which indicates *biologically imposed marginality. The Oxford English Dictionary*, s.v. "Marginal".

eighteenth century and used only when referring to the scribble on the margins of a piece of paper.[2] The *Dictionnaire de Trévoux* presents the term very literally : "*Marginal*...qu'on a mis où imprimé en marge. Ainsi, on dit un titre *marginal*, des notes *marginal*es."[3]

One can hardly underestimate the impact of Diderot's work in defining the term *marginality*, and his influence on his younger disciple, Rousseau. Denis Diderot was Rousseau's friend and mentor and greatly influenced society and his young colleague with his own writings. Moreover, Diderot's works are varied and interdisciplinary with pointed attempts to define what was marginal in his time.

Diderot was the Enlightenment's most able "definer" for he was not only an influential *philosophe,* but also the main editor and major contributor of the *Encyclopédie.* Diderot was an extraordinary observer of the use of language and defined many subtle aspects of the French language and literary idioms of the eighteenth century. He authored many articles in the *Encyclopédie*, and was its co-editor along with Jean le Rond d'Alembert. However, it is possible to conclude that neither Diderot nor d'Alembert conceived of a separate category for *les marginaux* as there is no reference whatsoever to a human condition called *"La marginalité"* in the *Encyclopédie*.

It is in Diderot's efforts to treat the subject of *marginality* that he validates his intention to manipulate the many layers of literary expression. He defines terms not only in the most literal ways such as in the *Encyclopédie*, but also by paradox, metaphor, and opposition. Nevertheless we must also conclude that Diderot works systematically as he endeavors to demonstrate and locate the actual societal

---

[2] This is according to the definition of *marginal* in the *Dictionnaire de Trévou.* xThe dictionary reflects the way the word was used in the eighteenth century *Dictionnaire de Trévoux* (Paris: Libraires Associés, 1752).

[3] *Dictionnaire de Trévoux*, s.v. "Marginal.".

margins. These processes were Diderot's early attempt to try to define what has become known in our modern era as *marginality.*

For the first order of proof it is necessary to look at the character depictions in his novels. Through the use of the epistolary form of narrative in *La Religieuse,* Diderot reveals his heroine Suzanne's feelings of alienation. In *Le Rêve de d'Alembert,* a dialogic piece with a philosophical base, he offers greatly detailed descriptions, in almost modern clinical terms, of human anomalies of nature and discusses social implications for these anomalies. It is a story of a dream recounted in dialogic form, which in turn produces the effect on the reader of a dreamlike and unraveled state. Diderot also speaks of marginalization in his theoretical composition the *Lettre sur les Aveugles,* with the example of the character Saunderson and his ideas on *genius.* In all of these writings, Diderot examines biological dysfunctions in relationship to *marginality* with clinical candor and includes them in his attempt at definition. Passion is the connection between *genius* and *marginality* and is defined in Diderot's speculative work. It is in his later pieces, the *Pensées sur l'interprétation de la nature* and the *Eléments de Physiologie,* where Diderot offers actual fragments of definition that come closest to modern day descriptions of *marginality.*

Diderot selected of a group of words that he used interchangeably and repeatedly to represent the notion of *marginality.* An examination of these patterns is key in understanding how he worked to develop this concept. French descriptive terminology (such as *genie, bizarre and décousu)* is used by Diderot in his various works in an effort to raise the reader's consciousness of the concept of the outsider. One popular example he uses often is the word *original* and in this description from *La Réfutation suivie de l'ouvrage d'Helvétius intitulé l'Homme* he makes a clear reference to the nephew: [4]

> Selon moi, un *original* est un être bizarre qui tient sa façon singulière de voir, de sentir et de s'exprimer son caractère. Si l'homme original n'était

---

[4] These examples among others are treated later in this study.

pas né, on est tenté de croire que ce qu'il a fait n'aurait jamais été fait, tant ses productions lui appartiennent.[5]

In the introduction to *Le Neveu de Rameau*, Diderot uses the word *original* in a sense similar to what is meant today by *marginal* : "Si vous le rencontrez jamais et que son originalité ne vous arrête-pas",[6] and "Je n'estime pas ses originaux-là".[7] These are not isolated examples; this is a term he will use time and again in the same context. Diderot's use of the word *original* is enshrined in the *Dictionnaire de Trévoux* and comes close to matching the modern definition of the word *marginal*:

> Original-se dit encore d'un dessin, d'un tableau qu'un peintre fait d'imagination, de génie, quoique chacune de leurs parties soient copiées d'après nature. Peinture "original" se prend en bonne et en mauvaise part, en bonne lorsque dans un tableau tout y est grand, singulièrement nouveau ; & en mauvaise, lorsqu'on n'y rencontre qu'une singularité bizarrement grotesque.[8]

In addition to the demonstration of the meaning of *original* in *Le Neveu de Rameau* and *La Religieuse*, and *La Réfutation suivie de l'ouvrage d'Helvétius intitulé l'Homme* the terms *génie* and *bizarre and décousu* are also explored in the fragments of the *Pensées sur l'interprétation de la nature* and the *Eléments de physiologie*.

---

[5] Denis Diderot, *La Réfutation suivie de l'ouvrage d'Helvétius intitulé l'Homme* (Paris: Classiques Garnier, 1962), 579.

[6] Diderot, *Le Neveu de Rameau*. Ed. Herbert Dieckmann. Œuvres Complètes. (Paris : Hermann, 1989), 32.

[7] Diderot, *Le Neveu*, 32.

[8] *Dictionnaire de Trévoux,* s.v. "Marginal" The general thrust of this definition relates to many aspects of *marginality*. Diderot went to great lengths to discuss organic dysfunctions, but he never went so far as to create an operational definition of what makes something or someone *marginal*.

Diderot attempted to define the all encompassing concept of *marginality*, and in so doing was able to address its process as well as to make an important contribution to our present understanding. The way in which the individual becomes *marginal* is, in other words, an examination of process. Often the *marginality* represented in Diderot's works can be likened to a type of imprisonment, or to an existence which entails a personal lack of liberty. I suggest that alienation in this sense serves only as a superficial description for an overall concept that Diderot was trying to grasp, define and finally articulate.[9] Indeed, Lionel Trilling in his influential book *Sincerity and Authenticity* credits Diderot with a key role in describing the origins of the modern day concept of social alienation: "For Diderot society is all in all, the root and ground of alienation, it is social man who is alienated man."[10]

In order to understand the concept of *marginality*, it is necessary to resist conflating it with such terms as *alienation*, and *the other*. They are used as code words in various modern disciplines to indicate a distance created between a society and one person or groups of individuals and have become commonplace words in literary theory and the social sciences. The process of marginalization might include being an "*other*" or might lay bare the various levels and degrees of *alienation*. These terms are meant to connote a person or persons who live their

---

[9] Jacob Stockinger. "Homosexuality in the French Enlightenment." *Homosexualities and French Literature*. Ed. Elaine Marks. Ithaca: Cornell UP., 1979. 167-69. This fact is documented extensively by Jacob Stockinger in his book, and relates literary testimonies of homosexuality as being a *marginalizing* force for an individual.

[10] Lionel Trilling, *Prefaces to the Experience of Literature* (New York: Harcourt Brace Jovanovich, 1981), 30. I would go farther than Trilling here and differentiate between *alienation* and marginalization, notions commonly conflated. The term *alienation* covers only a part of the concept of marginalization. I would suggest that alienation refers most properly to the *process* of being marginalized and that the term *marginal* should be restricted refer to the *position* of the person in relation to society. Put otherwise, *marginal* is a relational term, and refers to a person's position in relationship to the norm, while *alienation* put emphasis on the process of becoming marginalized. According to the Marxist theory, alienated man was not necessarily marginalized. He was alienated from his work but still part of a certain class in society. *Marginal* is what people can become once they are socially alienated.

lives apart from the germinal and vibrant groups or classes that constitute the mainstream of a given society. Nevertheless, *marginality* remains a much broader concept then those denoted by these terms.

Immanuel Kant (1724-1804) devoted much of his philosophical writing to the investigation of social norms and the issue of the alienation of the individual from society.[11] More recently, socio-political alienation is considered an aspect of the modern notion of *marginality* usually expressed in the economic displacement of an individual which consequently leads to a wider sense of alienation from a society. The term alienation in this context is seen as a subcategory of marginalization.[12] Alienation has social and individual consequences, which can be traced back to the original meaning of the term. Social alienation means an individual's estrangement from others and from the environment. Smaller groups can also be alienated from larger groups. This particular interpretation of alienation was conceived by Hegel in *Reason and History*. Here Hegel addresses the issue of how individuals become alienated from their work when they perform tasks that are against their nature:

> Thus the elements are made use of in accordance with their nature and cooperate for a product by which they become constrained. In a similar way the passions' purpose is in accordance with their natural destination and structure for law and order against themselves.[13]

---

[11] Immanuel Kant pursues a discussion of language, alienation and reason in his book, *Critique of Pure Reason*. Trans. Norman Kemp Smith. (New York: St Martins Press, 1965), 61-95.

[12] It was by studying Hegel that Marx first came across the concept of alienation. The alienation that Hegel referred to was heavily drawn from Rousseau's Social Contract theory that: "... in organized society the individual must forfeit a certain number of individual rights to the state as the representative of the collective interest of the community." Ernst Mandel and George Novack, *The Marxist Theory of Alienation* (New York: Pathfinder, 1974), 13.

[13].Mandel and George Novack, *Alienation*, 35.

At the turn of the nineteenth century, Hegel had read Goethe's translation of *Le Neveu de Rameau* and commented on it at length in his *Phenomenology of Spirit* (1807). In her discussion on Hegel and Diderot, Julia Simon comments that "...the concern over originality and genius arises at precisely the same moment when the bourgeois individual comes into being."[14]

After the Enlightenment, various philosophers began to focus on the concept of *marginality*. Significantly, Karl Marx later reinterpreted Hegel's ideas based on the individual and culture and incorporated it into in his economic theory of *Das Kapital*. Whereas Hegel believed that without universal culture there can be no individual, under the Marxist interpretation, individuals become estranged from others and from work because of the impact of industrialization and modernization. The socio-politically alienated person has become an accessory to the society by means of economic default.[15]

As the economic boundaries that encircled their society became more clearly defined, the *philosophes* writing against the backdrop of eighteenth-century France became ever more keenly aware of the many different forms of alienation.[16] In order to underscore the importance of this fact Robert Mauzi, in his preface to the Folio edition of *La Religieuse*, attributes Diderot with having contributed greatly to shaping definitions within society.   He ascribes to Diderot the

---

[14] Julia Simon, *Mass Enlightenment : Critical Studies Rousseau and Diderot.* (New York: SUNY Press. 1995).

[15] In this vein of reasoning a person is destitute and does not possess the means for personal betterment without help from the society. Of course reasons for being placed in this position vary from culture to culture.

[16] Michel Foucault discusses the history of the pursuit of definition in science and dis-tinction in language in his book *Les mots et les choses: une archéologie des sciences hu-maines.*(Paris : Gallimard, 1966), p.138-139. Here he names Diderot specifically in this discussion and cites him as being one of the main proponents of the movement to promote science and trans-form language. "A travers ces problèmes, et les discussions qu'ils font naître, c'est un jeu pour les historiens de reconstituer les grands débats dont il est dit qu'ils ont partage l'opinion et les passions des hommes leur raisonnement aussi.

formulation of the modern concept of alienation and neatly separates his works into three categories:

1)   *La Religieuse* nous parlerait de l'aliénation physique.
2)   *Le Neveu de Rameau* de l'aliénation sociale.
3)   *Jacques le Fataliste* de l'aliénation métaphysique. Nous découvririons ainsi   l'homme privé de sa liberté[17]

Robert Mauzi's description can be deepened by further investigation into the varied consequences of each type of alienation experienced by the individual characters. According to Mauzi for example, *social alienation* is played out in *Le Neveu de Rameau* when the nephew intentionally estranges himself from his own society and then again from his society of fools. While all these categories of physical, social, and metaphysical alienation accurately describe the different types of alienation depicted by Diderot's characters, the word alienation in these contexts lacks the attention to the process and the sense of being made trivial by being marginalized. It is the word *privé* in the third category which puts the above categorizations into question. Translated into English, the word *privé* literally means: "bereft of or deprived of." In this sense it can also be construed as: "separated from" because the nephew is also estranged by external forces.[18]

Marginality is a useful concept because it includes *alienation* and incorporates the idea of process. Building on Mauzi's initial study, I have separated Diderot's typing of characters and situations into three main categories with these more nuanced aspects:

1) *La marginalité subie* or the *forcibly* marginalized. In *forced* marginalization we see those people who are compelled by society to a

---

[17] Robert Mauzi, "Préface," in *La Religieuse*, Denis Diderot (Paris: Gallimard, 1974), 42.

[18] Harrap's French and English Dictionary translates this word as "bereft of." This gives the sense that something is separated from someone. *Harrap's French Dictionary*, s.v. "Privé".

position of inferior social status or impaired liberty. The character of Suzanne Simonin of *La Religieuse* is an example of marginalization imposed within a given milieu.

2) *La marginalité choisie*, or *self-imposed* marginalization. In *self-imposed* marginalization we see those who choose a particular type of personal alienation for one reason or another. Rameau's nephew, an example of *self-imposed marginality*, alienates himself from others. *Le Neveu de Rameau* clearly illustrates Diderot's interest in *marginality*, especially with regard to unusual or bizarre types; after all, the nephew is one of Diderot's most striking *originaux*. [19]

3) *La marginalité biologique* or *biological predeterminism*. This category includes those persons who are marginalized because of societal aversion to biological defects or, more precisely, those who have been deemed separate by nature. The Mother Superior of Arpajon, whose lesbian nature and unbalanced physical appearance separate her from the norm, offers an example of Diderot's conception of *biologically* or *physically imposed* marginalization and its psycho-social consequences. *Biologically imposed* marginalization includes those who cannot function within the norm due to a biological impairment.

The categories of *marginality* are not always mutually exclusive, and they share different traits and often overlap. Diderot's works often include and combine several forms of marginalization at a time, yet highlight different facets according

---

[19] This concept is similar to the term self-alienation which is elaborated upon by Julia Kristeva: Julia Kristeva, *Etrangers à Nous-Mêmes* (Paris: Gallimard, 1988), especially in her chapter on Rousseau and Diderot, 355-71. The difference between marginalized and *alienated* remains the same here as our discussion in Chapter Three on *Le Neveu de Rameau* will indicate: marginalization is a much broader term then *alienation* and this also includes different types of *self-alienation*. In order to avoid confusion I will refer to this category as the *self*-marginalized *person*.

to the needs of the text. For example, in *La Religieuse* the categories of *imposed* or *biologically predetermined* marginalization can be seen to overlap. One born with a congenital deformity that is not crippling could function in society, yet might be ostracized because of a difference in appearance. This represents a mix of *biologically imposed* and *forced* marginalization. The end result is the same: the individual or group suffers from rootlessness and from a feeling of being forced to exist apart from their fellow men and women. These three categories facilitate our understanding of the process by which individuals are alienated. While the terms *marginality* and *alienation* are often used interchangeably, each also carries a unique significance. The term *alienation*, when used by literary and ist theorists, connotes an individual who is pushed to the side. In addition, *alienation* in the Marxist sense always includes economic implications. The issue of an individual's belonging to a society is brought into focus in the Marxist interpretation[20]

Many of the questions posed by the Enlightenment philosophers derive from their contact with people from distant cultures and the issue of the *other* is a prime example. These questions often remain unanswered, as contact with other distant cultures was fairly difficult and limited at the time.[21] As distinct from *alienation,* it has been noted that today the term *other* is usually used in reference to a person or persons from foreign cultures who are perceived as different. The

---

[20] It was just this alienation of people as *citoyens* that became the starting point of Marx's philosophical, political, and social thought. It is clear that Marx derived his definition from Hegel's reading of certain eighteenth-century philosophers, specifically Rousseau and Diderot. The eighteenth-century philosophers were beginning to emphasize the notion of belonging. Rousseau, in particular, used the term *citoyen* frequently. We also find the term used often in the pages of the *Encyclopédie.* For further information regarding this particular aspect of Diderot's work see Arthur McCandless Wilson, *The Testing Years, Repr. of 1957 Ed. Diderot: The Testing Years* New York: Oxford University Press, 1972*).*

[21] In *Supplément au voyage de Bougainville* we see one example of the avid curiosity exhibited by the intelligentsia of the Enlightenment. This is also a clear and entertaining instance of Diderot's exploration of otherness. A priest arrives in Tahiti and is offered Tahitian hospitality (sex with the wife or daughters of the chief). This notion of hospitality is, of course, anathema to the priest, while all the Tahitians think he is strange for refusing such an offer. The priest finally gives in to the social and physical pressures and fully enjoys his native welcome.

concept of *otherness* is perplexing enough today to be at the forefront of literary and social research.

Current understandings of the term *marginality* also are informed by the popularization of what is considered *the other*. *Otherness* can be described as a personalized form of alienation and is therefore a subgroup when analyzing the concept of *marginality*. The notion of *otherness* was aptly defined by Tzvetan Todorov in his book *The Conquest of America*:

> I can conceive of these others as an abstraction, as an instance from any individual's psychic configuration, as the Other-other in relation to myself, to me or else as a specific social group to which we do not belong. This group can in turn be interior to society: woman for man, the rich for the poor, the mad for the "normal" or it can be exterior to society....[22]

This description covers sociological aspects of *marginality*, including a large part of the range of what *the other* means. The above description relates to the concept of *marginality* by touching on a behavioral aspect and delineating what is *other*.

A principal theme throughout both the speculative and the fictional works of Diderot is the constant questioning of whether or not individuals are born with certain innate behaviors, and if so, which ones. Does the decision to exist on the periphery of society and does the victimization, which ultimately occurs to those seen as *the other*, precede or follow the stigmatization? Diderot treated different aspects of *marginality* and used many and varied techniques to present his line of questioning.

Some examples that will be explored in depth in this book include the lesbian mother superior of *La Religieuse* who is *marginal* because of her sexual preference, and the Siamese twins in *Le Rêve de d'Alembert* who are deemed *marginal* because of their congenital anomalies. The broader category Diderot tried

---

[22] Tzvetan Todorov, *La Conquête de l'Amérique* (Paris: Seuil, 1982), 13.

to describe could be referred to, in today's terms, as the marginalized and would include those who are mentally distanced from society.[23] Rameau's nephew is alienated from his milieu. In this example, the door is shut and the physical margin created:

> Lui. Rameau, Rameau, vous avait-on pris pour cela ! La sottise d'avoir eu peu de goût, un peu d'esprit, un peu de raison. Rameau, mon ami, cela vous apprendra à rester ce que dieu vous fit et ce que vos protecteurs voulaient. Aussi l'on vous a pris par les épaules ; on vous a conduit à la porte ; on vous a dit, Faquin tirez. Ne reparaissez plus.[24]

The relationship portrayed above demonstrates a type of *marginality* and elucidates the meaning of "Enlightened Insanity." Ironically it is the central character in *Le Neveu de Rameau* who is "other". In addition, the nephew becomes progressively alienated from himself. The philosopher places himself in the privileged position of someone who is resting on a self-delineated margin; he is both the observer and interpreter.

Diderot's work has enjoyed a widespread readership in France, especially in the nineteenth and twentieth centuries. At the turn of the twentieth century, Freud, Marx and Nietzsche all greatly contributed to the evolution of the concept of *marginality*. The unique quality that Diderot exhibits for his time is his ability to demonstrate many different facets of our current understanding of this concept specifically through the function of his characters, and his explanations of experimental process in his speculative works.

Over time, *marginality* has come to refer not exclusively to the process of alienation, but now also extends to the movement of individuals and groups moving

---

[23] Mentally alienated is used in the sense put forth by the OED, rather than in the Marxist sense of alienated labor. *The Oxford English Dictionary*, s.v. "Alienation". See our previous discussion on the Marxist definition of alienation.

[24] Diderot, *Le Neveu*, 89.

to the margin. *Marginal* in French or English defines a category in our modern-day conceptualization and covers a broad semantic and cultural range. Further, *marginality* specifies the degree to which individuals or groups are marginalized. In conclusion, the term *marginal* is a precise and appropriate term useful to the context of early modern thought, as it encompasses the many different types of alienation underscored in the literature and philosophy of the age of Enlightenment. *Marginality* also differs from alienation because it offers a mental picture of a concrete position at which the character has arrived after the specific process of alienation as portrayed by a character, or more precisely, expressed by an author. The term *marginality* therefore, serves as an umbrella for a phenomenon that occurred at the beginning of the eighteenth century and has only now become fully acknowledged and integrated into political discourse. This heightened awareness is in no small way attributable to the group of *philosophes* of which Diderot was a part. More specifically, our modern concept of *marginality* evolved, in part, from eighteenth-century explorations in literature and philosophy.

Chapter Two
Foolery and Insanity:
Pathways to the Margin in *Le Neveu de Rameau*

Marginality runs as a leitmotif through every aspect of Diderot's writings. Of all the French philosophers writing during the Age of Enlightenment, he made the most comprehensive attempt to explore what is known today as *marginality,* for Diderot was intrigued by and obsessed with those individuals separated from society. The chapter that follows probes the background and context of Diderot's enigmatic work *Le Neveu de Rameau* by highlighting both his use of language within the historical framework and his creative use of literary tropes.

When speaking of Rameau's nephew, Foucault describes him as being *marginal* : "Il vit au milieu des formes de la raison, un peu en marge..."[25] The most compelling combination of concepts arises from this description: the nephew is *"au milieu"* and *"un peu en marge."* (This is in reference to the nephew's position in society.) *"Au milieu"* places the nephew at the center of society, accepting him as a positive force, while *"un peu en marge"* in this description indicates Foucault's ambivalence to suggest that Diderot's characterization presents the nephew definitively on the margins of society.

Le Neveu de Rameau was written in 1762, but the original copy was not found until 1891. It is now thought that after the censorship of the *Encyclopédie*, and the unconventional nature of the work itself, Diderot did not wish to publish or diffuse this work directly after having written it. The original copy manuscript of *Le Neveu de Rameau* was most likely left in Russia after Diderot had amassed the great collection of books and art in his position as head librarian for Catherine the Great. The copy was then read in the court in Russia and then passed into the hands

---

[25] Michel Foucault, *Histoire de la Folie à l'âge classique*, (Paris: Gallimard, 1972), 365.

of the German philosopher and writer Schiller who in turn passed it on to the great German Romantic writer Goethe. Goethe so appreciated the piece that he translated it into German in 1805; and thus it is from this German translation that the modern reader first came to know of this novel. The long lost French original version was rediscovered in 1891 by George Mondval when he happened upon the piece at a *bouquiniste* in Paris along the Seine, along with other papers that Diderot's daughter Angelique de Vandeul had collected. It is this original French edition that we read today.

Diderot's concept of *marginality* evolves from both the fictional and speculative arenas of his work, and his characters are depicted in combination with vivid descriptions of the dynamics of interpersonal relationships, often serving as metaphors for mental alienation. While the characters Diderot used to represent much of the concept of *marginality* are fictional, he based many of his depictions on personal experience. Diderot always stood with one foot on either side of the invisible boundary that defined the limits of society and indeed he saw himself as a *marginal* person, as evidenced by his report to his friend Melchior Grimm in 1762, documented by Arthur Wilson in his biography of Diderot:

> Socrates at the moment of his death was looked upon at Athens as we are looked upon at Paris. His morals were decried, his life calumniated, he was at the very least a turbulent and dangerous spirit who dared to speak freely of the gods...My friends, may we resemble Socrates in all things, just as his reputation resembled ours at the moment of his execution[26]

The self-comparison to Socrates demonstrates that Diderot held his own nonconformity dear, as if he were appointed to the position of observer. The stance taken by Diderot was that of the *café philosophe;* He represented the philosopher sitting alone and at a comfortable distance observing, describing and defining society and its norms.

---

[26] Wilson, *Diderot:The Testing Years* ,446. Here Wilson reproduces Grimm's report of Diderot's words.

As a *philosophe* on the boundary of society Jean-Jaques Rousseau sought the guidance of Diderot early in his career. He reached out to Diderot, who was to become both his friend and eventually, his enemy. Rousseau and Diderot both wrote extensively on the various aspects of the phenomenon of marginalization, but it was Diderot more than Rousseau who attempted to define *marginality* in his work. Diderot provides us with a great deal of evidence that he pondered the notion of *marginality*, particularly because of his relationship with Rousseau, who embodied the very spirit of the *marginal* personality. To Simon Schama, in his book *Citizens*, Rousseau's peculiarity is a point of fact:

> Rousseau's paranoid conviction that he was persecuted by jealous *philosophes* such as his erstwhile friend Diderot as well as Voltaire and Melchior Grimm, fed the alienation felt by many writers who believed themselves unappreciated by the literary establishment in Paris.[27]

Records of the collaborative nature of relationships between the *philosophes* and their friends and patrons exist in the forms of correspondence, and collaborative projects such as the *Encyclopédie*, and the *Salons*. In Diderot's time, the *philosophes* were hard at work analyzing, defining and collaborating on many significant projects, and many enjoyed each other's company. Most of the *philosophes* were considered outside the mainstream at one point or another.

Diderot and Rousseau were marginalized as philosophers, for in eighteenth century Europe, their intellectual and political views were not part of the mainstream. One could conclude that their mutual marginalization was one of many reasons for their friendship. Their early mutual fondness was demonstrated by Rousseau's long walk to Vincennes to visit with the imprisoned Diderot. Nevertheless, it is apparent that Diderot looked askance, in particular, at Rousseau's type of self-appointed distancing, as it left his friend far removed from the world. Diderot was unhappy with Rousseau's decision to become a recluse, as

---

[27] Simon Schama, *Citizens; A Chronicle of the French Revolution* (New York: Knopf, 1989), 160–1.

he was at odds with a number of Rousseau's personal and philosophical decisions. Diderot eventually begged Rousseau to put an end to their bitter arguments, but to no avail. Rousseau finally moved away from Paris, and when he did eventually return, he refused so much as to meet with Diderot.

Diderot began to feel more marginalized from society at the time of his estrangement from Rousseau. An outcast by choice, Diderot never reached the same degree of personal alienation as did his friend Rousseau. According to Diderot, Rousseau exhibited traits of paranoia early on in their relationship, and Diderot, on his part, expressed his alienated feelings from Rousseau by exploring different aspects of *marginality,* specifically within the context of his work *Le Neveu de Rameau.* In fact, his concern for Rousseau's mental status may have impacted more than a few of his writings[28]

Despite their similarities, the differences between the two philosophers' eccentricities were significant; Diderot was an occasional self-distanced observer, while Rousseau became an obsessive recluse. Diderot chose to remain on the margins as a critic and observer whereas Rousseau's intention however, was to detach himself completely, and as we have noted, to remove himself from the reaches of Parisian society. Clearly, in order to perform the role of observer, one must have some relationship, however minimal, with the society under scrutiny. Perhaps because of Rousseau's decision, the distinction between *forced* and *self-imposed marginality* holds such a prominent place in Diderot's work.

Rousseau was determined to separate himself from a society he found to be flawed, cruel and corrupt. Leo Damrosch aptly portrays Rousseau as the embodiment of the idea of the *marginal person* by emphasizing that Rousseau often displayed his uneven personality and how his erratic qualities affected his achievement:

---

[28] Wilson, *Diderot: The Testing Years* (New York: Oxford University Press, 1957), 104.

He stands as the type of lonely and questing spirit, but loneliness is not necessarily attractive and many people have found his personality exasperating. He was unreliable and temperamental, highly demanding of those around him, with a noble self-image that clashed with everyday behavior."[29]

Diderot's own feelings of marginalization, coupled with what he had witnessed in relation to his friends and family, became progressively evident in his work, though the degree of influence is impossible to quantify. The distanced position on the margins of society can be discerned from the famous opening lines of *Le Neveu de Rameau:*

Qu'il fasse beau qu'il fasse laid, c'est mon habitude d'aller sur les cinq heures du soir me promener au Palais Royal. C'est moi qu'on voit, toujours seul, rêvant sur le banc d'Argenson. Je m'entretiens avec moi-même de politique, d'amour, de goût ou de philosophie.[30]

Here the philosopher positions himself as an observer, alone and ready to ponder anything. This point is underscored by the following famous line from the first part of the dialogue when he says: *"mes pensées ce sont mes catins."*[31] His thoughts are his prostitutes and he has the freedom to follow them wherever they will take him.

The use of the role of the fool adds integral dimensions to the concept of the insane person's role and locates it within eighteenth-century context. The nephew does not have to be insane to be a fool and conversely he does not have to be a fool to be insane. Insanity and foolishness are two separate traits that the nephew exhibits and Diderot makes this distinction clear in a number of passages.

---

[29] Leo Damrosch, *Jean-Jacques Rousseau: Restless Genius* (Boston: Houghton Mifflin, 2005), 4.

[30] Diderot, *Le Neveu de Rameau,* 70.

[31] Diderot, *Le Neveu,* 70. The very image conjured by the word "catins," or "trollops" infers *marginality* on many levels. The philosopher follows a process of unraveling in order to arrive at the truth. This *unraveling* is discussed at length in Chapter Four.

Possessing both traits gives the nephew much more freedom in society. If he is deemed insane, his outlandish behavior is justified and he can do as he pleases. If he is merely the fool, he will be invited into certain circles to provide entertainment as in the fragment below. At this juncture the role of the fool is expressed in terms of ownership and his objectification is clear. The nephew's behavior causes him to become an object in the eyes of others. The position of being the *fou* is consciously associated with the social and artistic role of the court jester:

> Il n'y a point de meilleur rôle auprès des grands que celui de fou. Longtemps il y a eu le fou du Roi. Moi je suis le fou de Bertin et de beaucoup d'autres, le vôtre peut-être dans ce moment ; ou peut-être vous le mien. Celui qui serait sage n'aurait point de fou. Celui donc qui a un fou n'est pas sage ; s'il n'est pas sage il est fou ; et peut-être, fut-il roi, le fou de son fou.[32]

This honored position attributes high powers of perception and communication to the fool. The character depiction of *Lui* is presented as a person with limited psychological boundaries. He is therefore able to absorb and express more freely his non-normative social behaviors. He is without the self-consciousness or filters of socially-appropriate functioning. The nephew chooses to act differently than the norm, and as a consequence of the author's device, he represents diverse viewpoints.

The act of choosing one's behavior establishes the boundary between foolery and insanity. Though not necessarily insane because of the blurring of these margins, *Lui* is given a very important role, especially by *Moi*, the complacent, self-satisfied philosopher. *Lui* is a mouthpiece, an alter-ego, a sounding board, and an entertainer. He has the very position of being outside the *self* as he is constructed in opposition to *Moi*. As we read *Lui* we are therefore aware that the nephew is other than the self. One of the examples of Diderot's technique of mirroring begins here with the character of *Lui*, in fact one of his most important attributes is his

---

[32] Diderot, *Le Neveu*, 39.

ability to be self-reflexive. This allows the reader to reflect upon his behavior and to see it as abnormal, therefore paradoxically defining the norm. It is in this context that we see the philosopher-narrator excusing and even justifying the nephew's behavior by calling the nephew *fou*, yet we are aware from the conversations between *Moi and Lui*, that the nephew's behavior is of a more complex nature. All his behaviors are self-imposed barriers to his integration into society, a fact which paradoxically gives him a certain freedom of movement at the periphery.

French society in the eighteenth century was just beginning to address social deviation by locking away many men and women with various asocial behaviors. *Le Neveu de Rameau* was written in a time of growing social upheaval, when political prisoners were lumped together with criminals and the mentally unstable. It is well documented how the insane were summarily locked away with criminals. Here one sees that the insane were grossly misunderstood, and the institution of Bicêtre on the outskirts of Paris was the vile place to which they were relegated [33]:

> Trop grande lèpre pour le point de la capitale ! Le nom Bicêtre est un mot que personne ne peut prononcer sans que je ne sais quel sentiment de répugnance, d'horreur et de mépris. . . il est devenu réceptacle de tout ce que la société a de plus immonde et vil.[34]

Those who were mentally unstable were not separated from the criminals, therefore leaving questions as to whether society blamed the mentally ill for what might be their own biological destiny. The idea of uniformity was very much at the forefront as one important ingredient that defined the norm. This also demonstrates that society was far from understanding the differences in behaviors, let alone their etiologies.

---

[33] The fact that Bicêtre was (and is still) outside on the outskirts of Paris, puts the insane on the physical margin of the city.

[34] Here Stockinger is citing Mercier: Stockinger, "Homosexuality in the French Enlightenment," 168.

It is in this context that we see the philosopher-narrator excusing and even justifying the nephew's behavior by calling the nephew *fou*, yet we are aware from the conversations between *Moi and Lui*, that the nephew's behavior is of a more complex nature. All his behaviors are self-imposed barriers to his integration into society yet paradoxically give him a certain freedom of movement at the periphery. Foucault aptly contextualizes the nephew's asocial behavior as he looked at eighteenth century French society:

> Interroger le Neveu de Rameau dans le paradoxe de son existence si voyante et pourtant inaperçue au XVIIIe siècle, c'est se placer légèrement en retrait par rapport à la chronique de l'évolution ; mais c'est en même temps se permettre d'apercevoir, dans leur forme générale, les grandes structures de la déraison—celles qui sommeillent dans la culture occidentale, un peu au-dessous du temps des historiens.[35]

The passage above attests to a general need in Western culture to classify and quantify human behavior. The historical and cultural justification offered by Foucault is *Histoire de la folie à l'âge classique* explored the mentality of an age, giving definition to what constituted the mid-eighteenth-century concept of asocial behaviors and teased out definitions of insanity with historical documentation. In this recounting, Foucault even suggests early difficulties defining behavior and says that insanity was sometimes lumped together with leprosy:

> C'est donc dans le fantastique, non dans la rigueur de la pensée médicale, que la déraison affronte la maladie, et s'en rapproche. Bien avant que soit formulé le problème de savoir dans quelle mesure le déraisonnable est pathologique, il s'était formé, dans l'espace de l'internement, et par une alchimie qui lui était propre, un mélange entre l'horreur de la déraison et les vieilles hantises de la maladie. De très loin, les antiques confusions de la lèpre ont joué une fois encore ; et c'est la vigueur de ces thèmes fantastiques qui a été le premier agent de synthèse entre le monde de la déraison et l'univers médical.[36]

---

[35] Foucault, *Histoire de la Folie à l'âge classique*, 364.

[36] Foucault, *Histoire de la Folie à l'âge classique*, 377–8.

Society in the mid-eighteenth century was just beginning to confront the idea that mental behavior was a medical and biological issue. The mentally unstable were often confused with a wide range of *marginals* that included the physically challenged, the sexually deviant, the chronically ill and the criminally insane. The ambiguity of mixing foolery, illness and insanity continues today as lawyers and professionals in mental health fields still struggle to describe insanity and distinguish between acts committed by people who are not responsible for their own behaviors and those who should be held culpable. French society in the mid-eighteenth century was beginning to formulate an idea that there were neither differences between the criminal and the insane, nor between foolery and insanity. Yet beyond Foucault, there is little scholarship to date that can clearly describe the notion of insanity as it actually existed in the eighteenth century. All we can say is that there was a tendency to relegate all the *marginal* types together to prisons.

Later in the eighteenth century, (between 1780-1790) actual asylums were created for the mentally-unstable and yet the conditions were still like those of a prison. Not until this century have the mentally insane been regarded in a separate light from that of the criminal. The category of the criminally insane in this century covers a large range of behaviors, and still allows for the understanding of some criminal actions as being motivated by insanity.

It is tempting for the modern reader to consider the nephew as mad and at first consideration this might make perfect sense, especially since Diderot himself is constantly leading the reader to that perspective:

> Si vous le rencontrez jamais et que son originalité ne vous arrête pas ; ou vous mettrez vos doigts dans vos oreilles, ou vous vous enfuirez. Dieux quel terrible poumons. Rien ne dissemble plus de lui que lui même. Quelquefois, il est maigre et hâve, comme un malade au dernier degré de la consomption ; on compterait ses dents à travers ses joues. On dirait qu'il a passé plusieurs jours sans manger, où qu'il sort de la Trappe. Le mois suivant il est gras et replet, comme s'il n'avait pas quitté la table d'un financier, où qu'il eût été renfermé dans un couvent de bernardin. [37]

---

[37] Diderot, *Le Neveu*, 71. *Emphasis mine.*

In literature as in life appearances may be deceptive and this description of the nephew is not necessarily intended to be a portrait of madness. On this point, Diderot seems to be intentionally ambiguous in painting his portrait of the nephew as a bizarre individual and an eccentric. He is rather *raté* or failure. At times he is even grotesque, and is made to be repulsive to the reader. Diderot cleverly cloaks his character with ambiguity so that the reader is left with an idea rather than with a clear behavioral definition.

As readers, we are part of the reading process, as we identify with the Philosopher and with the nephew. Hurtful truths are once removed from our direct feelings because they are connected with what is considered *other*. Yet there are times when the *other* becomes the self: "Différents et complices, autres et mêmes, *Moi* et *Lui* s'opposent, s'entendent, échangent même leurs places. (Lui, effronté, prône brusquement la vertu...")[38]

What happens when the worlds of the philosopher and the crazy nephew collide? What occurs to the reader when this crossover takes place? The positions shift, and the reader is caught up in the dialectic. In this particular text the reader is rarely invited into the action rather, she is marginalized by most of the action taking place. By turns, it is the characters who are active in the foreground and then at times it is the readers who are active in the process of the dialogue. The characters interact by talking to themselves in a sort of mono-dialogue. This act suggests that, at times, there is no need for the reader actively to reflect and mirror responses because the philosopher answers the questions posed by the nephew and *vice versa*.

The most important issue for Diderot is that the truth is found in a state of being in which one is psychologically unraveled. The varied discourse that Diderot uses in this text demonstrates his attempt to unravel and deconstruct. The philosopher is close to the truth because he lets his mind wander. The nephew on

---

[38] Kristeva, *Etrangers*. 198, ellipsis original.

the other hand is even nearer to the truth because he exists in the raw emotional state where the truth is found.

As defined in the opening words of the novel, the worlds of the philosopher and the nephew are at first completely separate. The narrator speaks largely to himself. Here, the philosopher begins the dialogue as the narrator:

> Je m'entretiens avec moi-même de politique, d'amour, de goût ou de philosophie. J'abondonne mon esprit à tout son libértinage. Je le laisse maître de suivre la première idée sage ou folle qui se présente, comme on voit dans l'allée de Foy nos jeunes dissolus marcher sur les pas d'une courtisane à l'air éventé, au visage riant, à l'oeil vif, au nez retroussé, quitter celle-ci pour une autre, les attaquant toutes et ne s'attachant à aucune. Mes pensées ce sont mes catins.[39]

Whereas Diderot uses other stylistic formulations to create ambiguity, the metaphor here is clear, the philosopher who lets himself be led by his wildest thoughts is perverse, for wild thoughts are like prostitutes; they are mental trollops. The tone is of course a satirical one, and there is a difference between the philosopher's meanderings and the nephew's intense and bizarre wanderings.[40] Yet I suggest it is only a matter of degree, and the nephew dares to reach beyond the point where the philosopher will not go. In addition to this the nephew is also allowed to express his truths in a raw state, whereas the philosopher must organize his thoughts into a more coherent discourse. In *Le Neveu de Rameau* Diderot employs a dialogic style, a technique that agitates the reader and thus creates a literary/psychological margin from the start. As Lester Crocker insightfully comments:

> The use of the dialogue form is admirably suited to this effect. On the one hand, its free movement is conducive to randomness and the absence of linear structure. On the other hand, it allows a new dimensionality not found in either the confessional or the epistolary novel. The essential new dimension is that of confrontation, of immediate give-and-take. The theme

---

[39] Diderot, *Le Neveu*, 69.

[40] As indicated by the subtitle "Satyre Seconde."

of order and disorder, complex and elusive as Diderot contemplates it, is explored in its fullest reaches, cosmic social, and moral, as two antagonistic philosophical outlooks, embodied in the uncompromisingly complex and contradictory personalities of the antagonists, are pitted against each other.[41]

Along these lines in the *Dictionnaire de Diderot*, Roland Mortier defines the dialogic style in *Le Neveu de Rameau* as a reaction to the Socratic form of dialogue:

> A ce modèle classique s'oppose un dialogue authentiquement dialectique ou une pensée en affronte une autre et peut, à la limite, aller jusqu'à elle-même sans atteindre obligatoirement à une synthèse harmonieuse. Telle est bien la fonction du dialogue diderotien, où l'affrontement des points de vue vise avant tout à un approfondissement philosophique des opinions et à la prise en compte de leur diversité.[42]

The dialogic style itself in *Le Neveu de Rameau* produces a paradoxical effect. It is constructed to draw the reader into an intellectual experience while distancing her/him emotionally from the action. The function of Diderot's dialectical dialogic style is to expand on the Socratic style of debate that previously used irony and emotion as its source. This process is also explained under the title of dialogue by Roland Mortier in the *Dictionnaire de Diderot*:

> Il se présente le plus souvent sur le mode socratique, comme un dialogue de transmission, simple procédé derrière lequel se profile une pensée très élaborée, sûre d'elle-même et rapidement triomphante. La structure discursive la plus fréquente dans ce cas, est celle du débat entre le maître et le disciple. L'emploi du dialogue relève ici d'une rhétorique de la persuasion qui peut fonctionner sur le mode ironique ou sur celui de l'émotivité.[43]

---

[41] Crocker, *Chaotic*, 91.

[42] Roland Mortier and Raymond Trousson, eds., *Dictionnaire de Diderot* (Paris: Honoré Champion, 1999), 140.

[43] Mortier and Raymond Trousson, *Dictionnaire de Diderot*, 140.

Here Mortier likens Diderot's technique in describing Rameau's nephew to an animated and fragmented dialogue with a café philosopher. Mortier sees the dialogic style employed here by Diderot as a stylistic tactic deployed to emotionally distance and intellectually seduce the reader into the dialectic.

The dialogue between *Lui* and *Moi* excludes the reader, turning her into an observer and thus preventing any sort of psychological catharsis from taking place. The disharmony created by this dialectical style of communication exposes the reader to truths that can be appreciated at a non-cathartic and rational distancing.[44] Rameau's nephew is a case of *self-imposed marginality*, reinforced by the dialectical style of dialogue.

Alienation and the Nephew

The process of *alienation* as a sub-category of marginalization appears as a predominant theme in Diderot's work. As we have seen, the key character recognized by Diderot scholars as emblematic of the process of alienation is the nephew in *Le Neveu de Rameau*. *Le Neveu de Rameau* is a pivotal work because it clearly demonstrates that someone who "acts out," and whose behavior reflects his innermost thoughts, is treated as *marginal*. This behavior is at times likely to be labeled as insane, and perceptions that form as a result of reading and interpreting *Lui*'s "madness "define one form of *marginality*. *Le Neveu* does not fully explore the issue of insanity; rather, in order to demonstrate the nature of *self-imposed* marginalization, Diderot creates a character who uses insanity as one component of his multi-faceted personality. As Foucault says, the nephew's insanity is useful to his character:

> Confrontation tragique du besoin et de l'illusion sur un monde onirique, qui annonce Freud et Nietzsche, le délire du Neveu de Rameau est en même temps la répétition ironique du monde, sa reconstruction destructrice sur le théâtre de l'illusion : ' . . . criant, chantant, se démenant comme un forcené, faisant lui seul les danseurs, les danseuses, les chanteurs, les chanteuses,

---

[44] This type of emotional alienation can be also understood in the light of the theory of alienation as seen in the theater of Bertolt Brecht.

> tout un orchestre, tout un théâtre lyrique, se divisent en vingt rôles divers, courant, s'arrêtant avec l'air d'un énergumène, étincelant des yeux, écumant de la bouche. . . il pleurait, il criait, il soupirait, il regardait ou attendri ou tranquille ou furieux ; c'était une femme qui se pâme de douleur, c'était un malheureux livré à tout son désespoir, un temple qui s'élève, des oiseaux qui se taisent au soleil couchant. . . C'était la nuit avec ses ténèbres, c'était l'ombre et le silence.'[45]

In order to add richness to the character depiction of the nephew, Diderot portrays his insane disjunctive behaviors as the personality traits of a buffoon and a near-genius. Diderot's philosophical strategy in *Le Neveu de Rameau* is mapped out by his representations of these three compelling facets of *Lui's* personality, and each one of these parts of the nephew's personality contributes to the notion that he is a *self*-marginalized character. For example, *Lui's* share in the dialogue amounts to a process of destruction of the norms by which society strives to order itself—the very framework of values and of civilization.[46] *"C'est un composé de hauteur et de bassesse..."*in this all important phrase the nephew is represented as insane but also lucid, for as stated earlier, he is a composite, or *composé*. [47] The purpose of the nephew's behavior is to heighten the sense of *marginality* of the principal character.

It is also through the innovative character depiction of the nephew that Diderot merges the various types of *alienation* working together, thus making his character completely *marginal*. This portrait clarifies the distinction between the use of the terms *marginal* and *alienated*. The latter implies the action of pushing or removing oneself to the side of society, while *marginal* locates the position of one's existence while he/she is alienated. It is the position or function of the person who is alienated. The use of the term remains true in some capacity to its

---

[45] Foucault, *Histoire de la Folie à l'âge classique*, 369. Ellipses original. Foucault cites from the Plèiades edition of the *Neveu*.

[46] Crocker, *Chaotic*, 100.

[47] Diderot, *Le Neveu*, 70.

eighteenth-century meaning, which we find in the *Robert* under the heading: "Marge": "Dans une page, espace blanc autour du texte écrit ou imprimé."[48]

Moving from technique to terminology, let us now clarify the various labels given the nephew by Diderot in order to understand how the character depiction of the nephew helped in shaping the modern concept of social alienation and the broader concept of *marginality* as well. It is necessary to consider all of the wordplay in the use of appellations such as *original, fou, bouffon,* and *excentrique.* Diderot uses these terms among others to indicate the different marginalized positions that the nephew assumes as they take on special meaning in the context of Diderot's struggle to describe and explain the extreme social alienation of certain groups and individuals.

Original

It is noteworthy that the *Robert* cites this celebrated passage from *Le Neveu de Rameau* to contextualize and illustrate this use of *original*:

> Je n'estime pas ces originaux là…Ils m'arrêtent une fois l'an, quand je les rencontre, parce que leur caractère tranche avec celui des autres, et qu'ils rompent cette fastidieuse uniformité que notre éducation, nos conventions de société, nos bienséances d'usage ont introduite.[49]

The word *original* is not defined by Diderot in the *Encyclopédie* in this particular sense, yet he used the term repeatedly to denote *marginality*. The interpretation given by *Lui* of *Moi* in the above example taken from *Le Neveu de Rameau* represents the two sides of Diderot's personal dialectic and reflects a sense of introspective conflict. Let us return to the passage cited above to analyze with the aim of understanding where the bounderies of normal. The language used in the following passage especially : *"nos conventions de société,* nos bienséances d'usage ont introduite." is important in helping us to understand just where the

---

[48] Paul Robert, *Dictionnaire alphabétique et analogique de la langue française* (Paris: Le Robert, 1985), s.v. "Marge".

[49] Robert, *Dictionnaire alphabétique et analogique de la langue française*, s.v. "Fou".

margins of society lay. [50] The initial use of the plural *leur* indicates that there is more than one "Neveu" type person, and that there is a group wholly outside the norm. *Tranche* is a violent and abrupt word that gives weight to the action of separating from the norm. The use of the expression gives the idea that one is separated out from society, and the fact that "ils rompent cette fastidieuse uniformité" shows the intentionality behind the movement away from the norm. This highlights the point that the nephew is a self-fashioned *marginal* person. The word *uniformité* confirms the presence of a norm.

A fitting definition and a representation close to Diderot's use of the term *original* appear in *Dictionnaire Trévoux* in an eighteenth-century interpretation.

> On appelle ironiquement un original, un homme qui a quelque chose d'extravagant, de singulier et de ridicule dans ses manières ou dans son esprit.[51]

This description is one of many that point out the volatile and eccentric nature of Rameau's nephew. Not only is the word *original[ité]* used in this work to describe a *marginal* character, but in the very first description of the nephew cited above, Diderot uses it twice. *Original*, in more modern usage as recorded in the *Robert*, is synonymous with *excentrique and bizarre*:

> Marqué de caractères nouveaux et singuliers au point de paraître bizarre, peu normal. "*Il n'y a qu'en France que le mot original, appliqué à un individu soit presque injurieux.* (Gautier)[52]

Bizarre

Diderot also interchanges these terms and employs the word *bizarre* in his first poignant account of the nephew in this passage:

---

[50] Diderot, *Le Neveu*, 72. *Emphasis mine.*

[51] *Dictionnaire de Trévoux*, s.v. "Fou".

[52] Robert, *Dictionnaire alphabétique et analogique de la langue française*, s.v. "Original". The word original is also used in the same way in *La Religieuse*. See examples in previous chapter.

Un après-dîner, j'étais là, regardant beaucoup parlant peu, et écoutant le moins que je pouvais ; lorsque je fus abordé par un des plus *bizarres* personnages de ce pays où Dieu n'en a pas laissé manquer.[53]

In eighteenth century France, *fou* is also a synonym for the word *bizarre* and is used frequently to illustrate the personality of the nephew. Its meaning in this passage is explained in the *Trévoux*:

Fantastique, qui a des mœurs inégales, des opinions extraordinaires et particulières. *Morfus, tetricus, varius* Il est aussi subit. C'est un vrai bizarre au sens figuratif. Extraordinaire et hors de l'usage commun. C'est un homme bizarre, avec lequel on ne peut vivre.[54]

The use of *bizarre* as described in the above definition is pejorative, and relates to the idea of someone who does not act within the norm defined by society at the time.

Excentrique

In the eighteenth century the title of "crazy" was haphazardly assigned by some to what exists outside of our concept of "normative behavior." Julia Kristeva suggests that *excentrique* is even considered insane :

Excentrique sinon fou, le cynique nous montre *l'autre* de la raison ; étranger aux conventions, il se discrédite pour nous mettre en face de notre altérité inavouable. Ainsi au cynisme *haut*, aspirant à une mystique de la pureté humaine, se conjoint un cynisme *bas* qui—pour y parvenir (mais n'oublie-t-on pas souvent les fins quand on s'adonne aux moyens ?)—exhibe l'homme aliéné et dégradé.[55]

Additionally, the word *excentrique* in the eighteenth century exemplifies the idea of *marginality*: "Ex-center" means outside, but not necessarily crazy. Kristeva's use of the term *fou* here means *insane,* and when used in literature to define a fictitious character, raises a number of questions. The central issue is *how*

---

[53] Diderot, *Le Neveu*, 70.

[54] *Dictionnaire de Trévoux*, s.v. "Bizarre".

[55] Kristeva, *Etrangers*, 202.

to draw the line between innovation and insanity, as Foucault has done by separating *folie* from *déraison*. In this connection Bennett Simon, a practicing psychoanalyst who devotes much of his time to the teaching of psychoanalysis in literature, observes:

> Every culture, to my knowledge, has some category that can be called "madness," but madness is not always easily distinguished from other categories of thought and behavior. Further problems occur in separating madness from states of disturbance that occur in connection with particular life events or stages of life: sickness, separation, death, adolescence, old age, and so on. Generally speaking, each culture has rough limits of acceptable behavior in these situations, but when does profound grief become pathological mourning? Where does adolescent turmoil end and schizophrenia begin?[56]

Simon's explanation also sheds light on several aspects of the problem in labeling the nephew as a madman and gives us some insight into this difficulty and the problems the concept of insanity has presented through the history of literary interpretation. The issue that is underscored here is one of culture and its norms, which Diderot calls *conventions*, where uniformity of behavior is essential, especially in old regime French society.

Diderot reminds us that the nephew *acts* in a crazy manner to insure his marginalization, and he impels the reader this remember this at each juncture in the work. One must be careful to understand the mixed standards that color our reading of this text.

Génie

The alienated individual is also likely to be a person who possesses the extraordinary qualities of genius. Genius is found in the process of being, but for *Lui* genius is revealed in the process of the destruction of norms. In essence, this destruction is also a form of deconstruction and can be paralleled with Diderot's

---

[56] Bennett Simon, *Mind and Madness in Ancient Greece: The Classical Roots of the Modern* (New York: Cornell University Press, 1978), 31.

formulations about truth. In *Le Neveu de Rameau* as well as other important works such as *Le Rêve de d'Alembert* and *La Religieuse*, truth is found in the midst of bizarre behaviors and delirium, along the alleyways of irrationality and ambiguity. In *Le Neveu de Rameau*, the figure of *Lui* equates truth with beauty, and *Moi* rips this equation apart by saying that truth does not represent conventional morality. In this passage, for example, it is interesting to note the idea of self-alienation. This is an arena in which the nephew finds not only talent but genius. Diderot dances around a definition of genius by mentioning all the attributes that are not constituent to it. Here we are presented with yet another of Diderot's paradoxes:

> Lui. Je ferais comme tous les gueux revêtus ; je serais le plus insolent maroufle qu'on eût encore vu. C'est alors que je me rappellerais tout ce qu'ils m'ont fait souffrir ; et je leur rendrais bien les avanies qu'ils m'ont faites. J'aime à commander, et je commanderai. J'aime qu'on me loue et l'on me louera. J'aurai à mes gages toute la troupe vilmorienne ; et je leur dirai, comme on me l'a dit, Allons faquins qu'on m'amuse et l'on m'amusera ; qu'on me déchire les honnêtes gens et on les déchirera, si l'on trouve encore ; et puis nous aurons des filles ; nous nous tutoierons, quand nous serons ivres ; nous nous enivrerons ; nous ferons des contes ; nous aurons toutes sortes de travers et de vices. Cela sera délicieux. Nous prouverons que de Voltaire est sans génie ; que Buffon toujours guindé sur des échasses, n'est qu'un déclamateur ampoulé ; que Montesquieu n'est qu'un bel esprit ; nous reléguerons D'Alembert dans ses mathématiques ; nous en donnerons sur dos et ventre à tous ces petits Catons, comme vous, qui nous méprisent par envie ; dont la modestie est le manteau de l'orgueil, et dont la sobriété est la loi du besoin. Et de la musique ? C'est alors que nous en ferons.[57]

The nephew is a near genius at acting crazy and at playing the "fool." The true genius stands out on his own, whereas the nephew must act the clown in order to be recognized. This idea presents another of Diderot's paradoxes: the nephew is in control of his *marginality* and chooses the role of the fool in order to be noticed, yet when he is noticed, his real life seems to the reader more mediocre than ever. The nephew is only noticed in relationship to being a *raté* or failure and therefore

---

[57] Diderot, *Le Neveu*, 112–3.

he does not prove to be an "all around genius." He is more like an "idiot savant" in this respect. He thus asserts his own individuality through perfecting his own truly *marginal* behavior. Here is our first encounter with him:

> Un après-dîner, j'étais là, regardant beaucoup, parlant peu, et écoutant le moins que je pouvais ; lorsque je fus abordé par un des plus bizarres personnages de ce pays où dieu n'en a pas laissé manquer.[58]

In this portrait, the nephew looks and acts in a peculiar manner. We are soon to understand that the nephew's way of coping with his own mediocrity becomes a way of life, that is to say he constantly finds ways to be singled out. *Le Neveu de Rameau* represents Diderot's exploration into the psychosomatic basis of insight and the act of artistic genius.

In his article "The Theme of Genius in *Le Neveu de Rameau*," Fellows describes the idea of genius that is expressed throughout Diderot's work. A genius is someone who "must express inner urges ignoring all other considerations, and insisting on its achievement."[59] The nephew certainly shows signs of expressing his inner urges, but to what end? He is a failure. *Moi* constantly points out this fact to the nephew. Yet the nephew blames fate and environment for his failures.

Rameau's nephew exhibits is a muddled persona, and this is an example of how various forms of *marginality* may overlap and interact within individual characters. In this situation, it is useful to recall the distinctions between the three different types of *marginality: forced, self-imposed* and *biologically predetermined*, which appear in Diderot's works. It is equally significant to consider the point that though different, these forms are not always distinct, nor are they always presented separately. Rameau's nephew is an example of *forced* marginalization and at the same time is characterized as acting of his own free will. But within the perspective

---

[58] Diderot, *Le Neveu*, 70.

[59] Here, too, we gain insight into Diderot's linkage of determinism to the idea of genius. For more on this topic see: Otis Fellows, "The Theme of Genius in Diderot's *Neveu de Rameau,"* *Diderot Studies* II (1952): 168–99.

of *self-imposed* marginalization, the nephew's rejection is complete. Instead of trying to fit into the mainstream, he tells us again and again how adept he is at *not* fitting in. Thus in the following line Diderot emphasizes the point that this character is an example of *self-imposed marginality*: "Je faisais le fou. On m'écoutait. On riait. On s'écriait, il est toujours charmant".[60]

Key to the typology of *marginality* is the idea of *process*. Each step in the process of marginalization is represented in some way, not only in *Le Neveu de Rameau*, but also in subsequent works of Diderot. When the issue of *self imposed marginality* arises in *Le Neveu de Rameau*, so does the question of *biologically predetermined* marginalization. Like the blind person Saunders of the *Lettre sur les Aveugles*, who is able to feel things a sighted person might not, the insane person is able to form thoughts the ordinary person might not. Each of the *marginal* types contributes to an organic whole as part of the totality of *Le Neveu de Rameau*.

The long evolution of the concept of *marginality* from the eighteenth century to our own time can be traced back to the seminal work of Diderot. Once again we turn to Foucault's discussion of Rameau's Nephew in *L'Histoire de la folie à l'âge classique*, as he describes how the nephew has pre-figured not only Hegel, but has continued to influence post-Hegelian thought.

> Le rire du Neveu de Rameau préfigure à l'avance et réduit tout le mouvement de l'anthropologie du XIXième siècle ; dans toute la pensée post-hégélienne, l'homme ira de la certitude de toute la pensée à la vérité par le travail de l'esprit et de la raison ; mais depuis bien longtemps déjà, Diderot avait fait entendre que l'homme est incessamment renvoyé de la raison à la vérité non-vraie de l'immédiat, et ceci par une médiation sans travail, une médiation toujours déjà opérée du fond du temps.[61]

---

[60] Diderot, *Le Neveu*, 107. It is this self-awareness that exemplifies the idea of recognition or *anagnorisis*.

[61] Foucault, *Histoire de la Folie à l'âge classique*, 370.

The Parasite

Foucault prefigures the discussion of the *marginal* as a parasite. Michel Serres, in *Le Parasite*, gives a definition that seems to parallel Diderot's concept of a parasite. In the case of eighteenth-century society the marginalized individual might figure as a parasite living off society, producing nothing and contributing nothing. Serres describes Tartuffe as alienated from society in his description of Molière's famous character who is a flamboyant hypocrite and imposter: "Tartuffe est observateur, il est analyste. Introduit d'abord, inclus partout, retire à la fin où exclu, il est en position de catalyseur. Il paralyse, il analyse, il catalyse."[62]

Tartuffe serves as a reference for some aspects of marginality that Diderot draws upon. Tartuffe, like the nephew, draws attention to himself and is expert at manipulating a situation. It should be noted that Serres is not the first to make this comparison. Rameau's nephew has often been compared to Tartuffe. Serres is expanding on an observation made by Diderot himself:

> Quand je lis le *Tartuffe*, je me dis : sois hypocrite, si tu veux ; mais je ne parle pas comme l'hypocrite. Garde des vices qui te sont utiles ; mais n'en aie ni le ton ni les apparences qui te rendraient ridicule.[63]

In the above passage, Diderot arranges a comparison in the form of a paradox; the nephew is similar to Tartuffe, but he is depicted with different intentions. The nephew is not the same kind of hypocrite as Tartuffe because he can pretend not to be, for he is a talented liar. In direct opposition to this, the nephew also finds situations to say what he means at all costs. These two methods of communication comprise parts of the process that alienates the nephew further from society. Foucault also compares the nephew to Tartuffe and emphasizes the fact that the nephew says what he means:

---

[62] Michel Serres, *Le Parasite* (Paris: Grasset, 1980), 221.

[63] Diderot, *Le Neveu*, 107.

Le Neveu de Rameau a faim et il le dit. Ce qu'il y a de vorace et d'éhonté chez le Neveu de Rameau, tout ce qui peut renaître en lui de cynisme, ce n'est pas une hypocrisie qui se décide à livrer ses secrets ; car son secret justement est de ne pouvoir pas être hypocrite : le Neveu de Rameau n'est pas l'autre côté de Tartuffe ; il manifeste cette immédiate pression de l'être dans la déraison.[64]

In Foucault's analysis Diderot attempted to distinguish between the two characters who shared certain traits. The nephew's frankness is due to his volatile nature. Moreover, he says things without premeditation. He eventually lets down his mask in his dialogue with *moi,* whereas in Moliere's play, we see the masked *Tartuffe*. The nephew is especially like Tartuffe in one aspect in particular, for he plays an active part in his own alienation process. Social, cultural, and perhaps even biological factors reinforce the nephew's self-alienation. *Le Neveu de Rameau* also examines in detail why some individuals decide to reject the mainstream and the mediocrity it may represent. In this passage we see that the nephew is alienated even from his own group of *marginal* personalities:

J'étais leur petit Rameau, leur joli Rameau, leur Rameau le fou, l'impertinent, l'ignorant, le paresseux, le gourmand, le bouffon, la grosse bête. Il n'y avait pas une de ces épithètes familières qui ne me valût un sourire, une caresse, un petit coup sur l'épaule, un soufflet, un coup de pied, à table un bon morceau qu'on me jetait sur mon assiette. Hors de table une liberté que je prenais sans conséquence ; car moi, je suis sans conséquence. On fait de moi, avec moi, devant moi, tout ce qu'on veut, sans que je m'en formalise ; et les petits présents qui me pleuvaient ? Le grand chien que je suis ; j'ai tout perdu ! J'ai tout perdu pour avoir eu le sens commun, une fois, une seule fois en ma vie ; ah si cela m'arrive jamais ![65]

Here one sees clearly the nephew's testament to the manner in which his own unbridled tongue makes him an outcast even from the society of outcasts, thus emphasizing his *marginality* from his own *marginal* group. The objectification of the nephew is clear, for he is used by the others. Yet as he states, this process gives

---

[64] Foucault, *Histoire de la Folie à l'âge classique*, 367.

[65] Diderot, *Le Neveu*, 88.

him a sort of liberty, and it is a path that he has chosen. The position is self-imposed and the movement to the margin is carried out.

Depicting the nephew as insane adds dimension to the character, and thus brings the reader closer to truths that might otherwise remain inchoate. Diderot's first texts on biological differences used blindness, deafness and the inability to speak as allegories; why not include insanity, too?[66]

Jeffrey Mehlman employs the cataract as the central metaphor in his discussion of *Le Neveu*. For Mehlman, a cataract is to the eye as *déraison* is to the mind.[67] Mehlman's simile goes only so far, because it is difficult to consider the nephew solely as someone who is born with a biological predisposition to insanity. I suggest that the form of *marginality* presented in *Le Neveu de Rameau* is similar to others that Diderot has explored elsewhere, because here, too, quirkiness appears to be due to a combination of causes. For the *Neveu*, not to fit in means to be different. Diderot ensured that the nephew was different enough in every way to underscore the central, albeit unannounced, theme of marginalization. The nephew exhibits his idiosyncratic behavior with full awareness. He professes here that he behaves in a crazy manner of his own free will: "Hors de table une liberté que je prenais sans conséquence; car moi, je suis sans conséquence".[68] The nephew is marginalized because of a set of circumstances that are entirely within his control; in addition, his behavior is not without personal consequence. The nephew acts the fool so as to draw attention to himself; at this point he is aware of his own mediocrity, and being the fool will set him apart from the other company.

For the nephew, negative attention is better than no attention. Each facet of the nephew's fragmented existence can be said to act as a part of the plan of

---

[66] I am referring here to *La Lettre sur les Aveugles* and *La Lettre sur les Sourds et Muets*.

[67] Jeffrey Mehlman, *Cataract: A Study in Diderot* (Middletown, CT: Wesleyan University Press, 1979).

[68] Diderot, *Le Neveu*, 88.

self-marginalization that the author plotted out for him. Diderot also points out there would be consequences if the nephew were to conform, highlighted by the sarcasm of *Moi* :

Moi. Et pourquoi employer toutes ces petites viles ruses-là [?][69]

Lui. Viles ? Et pourquoi, s'il vous plaît. Elles sont d'usage dans mon état. Je ne m'avilis point en faisant comme tout le monde. Ce n'est pas moi qui les ai inventées ; je serais bizarre et maladroit de ne pas m'y conformer...[70]

The context of this exchange is significant as *Moi* has just asked *Lui* why he needs to use deceptions to get his way. He (*Lui*) is justifying his outrageous behavior by saying that this is what people have come to expect of him. The nephew's company is desired in his present state, because he serves as a type of entertainment. Foucault stresses this view in *L'Histoire de la folie* :

Ce qui n'était que bouffonnerie dans le personnage *dérisoire* de l'hôte importun, révèle, au bout du compte, un imminent *pouvoir de dérision*. L'aventure du Neveu de Rameau raconte la nécessaire instabilité et le retournement ironique de toute forme de jugement qui dénonce la déraison comme lui étant extérieure et inessentielle.[71]

The nephew's behavior may be immoral, and the "truths" that he espouses do seem outrageous, but these are the wishes and desires that most people subconsciously harbor. *Lui* differs in that he has the requisite audacity to forgo morals and blurt out his wishes with no boundaries or cares attached; he possesses no social filter.

Foucault's theory reflects the notion that the nephew presents a marked distinction between foolery and insanity in the eighteenth century. Parts of this theory are key in understanding the composite and *marginal* nature of the nephew's

---

[69] Diderot, *Le Neveu*, 109. Punctuation added by editors.

[70] Diderot, *Le Neveu*, 109.

[71] Foucault, *Histoire de la Folie à l'âge classique*, 365.

personality. If the nephew were to be considered insane, or simply a fool, he might not be the strongest example of *marginality* in Diderot's work, but it is just this combination that shows Diderot's ability to describe the social consequences of alienation. There is a sense of existence on the periphery, and of serving a purpose there. As Lester Crocker confirms, Diderot created this character as a reflection of the totality of his "chaotic order."[72]

The Nature of Genius

Diderot not only had a great interest in exploring the idea of genius, but also admired people who exhibited the qualities of genius. In fact the ordinary or mediocre person is consistently referred to in negative terms throughout Diderot's works and especially in *Le Neveu de Rameau*.[73] The tone of this little exchange is but one example where Diderot differentiates between talent and genius:

> Moi. Mais à quoi bon ce talent ?
> Lui. Vous ne le devinez pas ?
> Moi. Non. Je suis un peu borné.[74]

In pondering the nature of genius, Diderot comes to the conclusion that the concept encompasses much more than talent. His idea incorporates the notion that a genius is expected to behave differently from others. Arthur Wilson accurately underscores this intention:

> *Le Neveu de Rameau* is not a discussion merely about ethics; it is also an exploration of the nature of genius and of the mystery of creativity, and of the relationship between genius and morality, of whether genius can be developed, of whether it can be forfeited. All this covers new ground, for the older view of genius had thought of it as simply talent carried to a higher exponential power, whereas Diderot defines genius as a gift of nature differing from talent not in degree but in genius and pretends that he does not want it, it becomes evident that in reality he wants nothing more. What

---

[72] This term was coined by Crocker. Lester Crocker, *Diderot's Chaotic Order* (Princeton: Princeton University Press, 1974).

[73] See addendum and article in the *Encyclopedie*: Diderot, *Encyclopédie*, s.v. "*Génie*".

[74] Diderot, *Le Neveu*, 125.

the nephew has is talent, not genius. What he has is the capacity to perform, not the capacity to create.[75]

It is evident that Diderot was not convinced that genius was predetermined by biology, for *Lui* responds in the very next lines in the text: *"L'expression est de génie."* Herbert Dieckmann also clarifies the meaning of this expression in his article entitled "Diderot's Conception of Genius":

> The French language has created two expressions which, when used, precisely, show two fundamentally differing conceptions of genius: *Avoir du génie* and *être un génie* or *un homme de génie*. The term means nothing more than to possess great talent.[76]

Dieckmann pursues his exploration of Diderot's notion of genius by differentiating talent from genius. Thus the nephew possesses great talent, yet falls short of being a genius, and succeeds only at being a fool. He does not follow in the footsteps of his uncle, the great court composer Rameau. This work expresses the notion people could have a predisposition to genius and then later develop it.

The transition from the conception of genius as mere talent to the conception of *the genius* as an individual was accomplished through a specific act of thought.[77] Diderot's character assumes many different postures. Not only does he act insane, but he is also a fool, as Foucault comments on Lui's self-description : "Il est fou parce qu'on lui a dit qu'on l'a traité comme tel : 'On m'a voulu ridicule et je me le suis fait'"[78]

The same word *fou* is used for both *être fou*, which is close to *déraison* in meaning, and *fou* (as in *folie*) which bears more the sense of buffoon. These are two markedly different roles, and sometimes they seem conflated. Yet what these

---

[75] Wilson, *The Testing Years (Repr. of 1957 Ed. Diderot: The Testing Years)*, 420.

[76] Herbert Dieckmann, *Cinq Leçons sur Diderot* (Geneve: Librairie Droz, 1959), 152.

[77] Dieckmann, *Cinq*, 152.

[78] Foucault, *Histoire de la Folie à l'âge classique*, 363.

classifications have in common is more to the point: both positions are *marginal* and both in this particular context are self-imposed. Another term, *déraison*, is used interchangeably with the word *folie* as Foucault explains:

> La déraison en lui est toute de surface, sans autre profondeur que celle de l'opinion, soumise à ce qu'il y a de moins libre, et dénoncée par ce qu'il y a de plus précaire dans la raison. La déraison est tout entière au niveau de la futile folie des hommes. Elle n'est rien d'autre peut-être que ce mirage.[79]

While the thinkers of the Age of Enlightenment could not consciously have anticipated the theories of Freud, they did take the first steps toward the evolution of ideas of which marginalization was the base. Diderot, among others, helped to point out that people were marginalized because of various factors, one of them being behavior that is defined as deviant. As Foucault, says, "Le Neveu de Rameau, lui, sait bien-et ce qu'il y a de plus obstiné dans ses fuyantes certitudes-qu'il est fou"[80]

Rameau's nephew could serve as an example of what it meant to be insane because he acts the fool. But as Foucault warns us, we need to look very closely at the text before we make a judgment.

> Cette conscience d'être fou, elle est bien fragile encore. Ce n'est pas la conscience close, secrète et souveraine, de communiquer avec les profonds pouvoirs de la déraison ; le Neveu de Rameau est une conscience serve, ouverte à tous les vents et transparente au regard des autres.[81]

As already noted, twentieth first century instinct would be to separate insanity from foolery. But in the eighteenth-century French context the task is more ambiguous. Since modern biological and psychological concepts of insanity did not exist in Diderot's time, posing the question of what the author is trying to

---

[79] Foucault, *Histoire de la Folie à l'âge classique*, 361.

[80] Foucault, *Histoire de la Folie à l'âge classique*, 363.

[81] Foucault, *Histoire de la Folie à l'âge classique*, 361.

convey by depicting a psychically chaotic character is a more appropriate approach. If we examine the author's own terminology, we see a type of madness defined in the terms with which Diderot has Rameau's nephew describe himself:

> "Vous savez que je suis un sot, un ignorant, un fou, un impertinent, un paresseux, ce que nos Bourguignons appellent un fieffé truand, un escroc, un gourmand. . ."[82]

These terms, *sot, impertinent,* and so on, all describe non-conformist behavior on some level. The word *fou* is used here again, as *un fou*, thus clarifying the meaning as a fool or *bouffon*. In this case it is apparent that the nephew describes nephew describes his behaviors with a language of awareness and clarity, almost as an act of defiance. It is obvious that he is a fool, yet being defiant by acting foolish does not constitute insanity. Heather Arden, a scholar in Medieval French literature, delves into the history of the term *fou* in her book *Fools Plays; A Study of Satire in the Sottie.*

> The term *fou* originally applied to the licentious character, who had the right to say whatever he chose, as he is found in the *Fête des Fous* and the mysteries. The term slowly evolved to the point where it designated the "wise fool," the omnipresent and omniscient fool situated outside the group, who comments in an ironic manner on the behavior of others (as in *Le Povre Jouhan*). At this point, when the *fou* has the characteristics of wisdom and frankness, without those of licentiousness and buffoonery, the character becomes the *sot* of the *sottie...*[83]

Diderot was likely influenced by early depictions of the *fou* in creating the nephew character. The word *fou* in this particular context is used most often in connection to the nephew's madness or *folie*. In seeking a definition we must be

---

[82] Diderot, *Le Neveu*, 87, ellipsis original.

[83] Heather Arden, *Fools Plays: A Study of Satire in the Sottie* (London: Cambridge University Press, 1980), 41. A valuable discussion of the importance of the role of the fool in medieval French literature can be found there as well.

aware of the fact that to our modern sensibilities, *le fou* is different than *être fou*. In the eighteenth century this definition was applied to *le fou*:

> On dit familier qu'un *fou* en amuse bien d'autres, lorsque plusieurs personnes s'arrêtent à voir ou entendre quelques bagatelles.[84]

The above definition confirms Arden's contention that *un fou* was more of a jester than an insane or witless person, and filled a particular social or literary role. The modern reader must exercise caution in encountering the term *fou* lest one incorrectly read insanity into *Le Neveu de Rameau*.

The position of the nephew is elevated because his behavior becomes objectified. Foucault also speaks of insanity in tandem with the position of the fool rather than identifying it as a separate, fragmented part of the nephew's personality. It is appropriate to read the *bouffon* or the fool as a separate facet of the nephew's complicated personality. There is a progression and a connection in the separate behaviors from the fool to an insane person. The fool as we have established is an object. *Moi* calls him "*mon fou.*" Another related term in Diderot's work is the word *fou,* in the works of Diderot it is often used interchangeably with *original*.

Lester Crocker expresses the view that: "*Le Neveu de Rameau* is a drama of identity, *Lui* does not know who he is or who he wants to be, or perhaps who he can be".[85] I take issue with Crocker here. The nephew knows full well who he is. In fact he is in a comfortable place: the in between, not quite the fool, not quite crazy. He is depicted with precise intentionality, which "acting crazy" infers. Most people who are deemed "insane" do not intend to be insane. Kristeva states that the nephew's choice to be considered insane therefore shows a marked level of sanity:

> Le Neveu de Diderot *ne veut* pas se ranger—il est l'esprit du jeu qui ne veut pas s'arrêter, ne veut pas pactiser, mais ne veut que provoquer, déplacer, inverser, choquer, contredire.[86]

---

[84] *Dictionnaire de Trévoux*, s.v. "Fou".

[85] Crocker, *Chaotic*, 93.

[86] Kristeva, *Etrangers*, 198.

Though Kristeva often refers to the nephew as crazy, she also underscores the intentionality of the character's actions. The actions are voluntary, thus the use of the verb *vouloir*. *Volonté* on the part of the nephew also gives him the clarity of mind to imitate psychotic behavior. This is where the nephew exhibits greatness.

> Qui est le Neveu? L'adversaire du philosophe ou sa face cachée ? L'autre opposé ou le double nocturne qui fait surface ? Une réponse tranchée à cette question mettrait fin à la pantomime et trahirait les "pensées catins" que Diderot, dans une envolée polyphonique inouïe, met précisément en scène par l'affrontement entre Moi-philosophe et Lui-étrange.[87]

Not unlike Foucault's distinction between *folie* and *déraison*, Freudian psychoanalysis separates between psychosis and neurosis.[88] In Freudian psychology, recognition of the difference between reality and the world of delusion is the difference between the psychotic and neurotic person. It has taken over two hundred years for Western culture to arrive at even a loose distinction on what is

---

[87] Kristeva, *Etrangers*, 198.

[88] Inherent in the idea that the nephew is insane is the notion that Diderot's portrait of the nephew can be interpreted as a scientific model for Freudian thinkers and especially those who strive to differentiate between neurosis and psychosis. The concept of *marginality* has most recently been adopted by Freudian thinkers in relationship to mental instability and mental illness. These definitions taken from the *Vocabulaire de la Psychanalyse* help clarify the separate definitions:

> a) En clinique psychiatrique, le concept de psychose est pris le plus souvent dans une extension extrêmement large de sorte qu'il recouvre toute une gamme de maladies mentales, qu'elles soient manifestement organogenétiques (paralyse générale par exemple) ou que leur étiologie dernière reste problématique (schizophrénie par exemple).
> b) En psychanalyse, on ne s'est pas donné d'amble pour tâche d'édifier une classification qui porterait sur la totalité des maladies mentales dont la psychiatre a à connaître; l'intérêt s'est porté

d'abord sur les affectations le plus directement accessibles à l'investigation analytique et, à l'intérieur de ce champ plus restreint que celui de la psychiatre, les distinctions majeures sont celles qui établissent entre les perversions, les névroses et les psychoses.

Dans ce dernier groupe, la psychanalyse a cherché à définir différentes structures: paranoïa (où elle inclut d'une façon assez générale les affectations délirantes) et schizophrénie d'une part; d'autre part mélancolie et manie. Fondamentalement c'est dans une perturbation primaire de la relation libidinale à la réalité que la théorie psychanalytique voit le dénominateur commun des psychoses, la plupart des symptômes manifestes (construction délirante notamment) étant des tentatives secondaires de restauration du lien objectal. Jean Laplanche and J-B. Pontalis, *Vocabulaire de la Psychanalyse* (Paris: Presses Universitaires Françaises, 1967), s.v. "Psychose".

considered criminal and what is considered insane. The distinction between what is psychotic or neurotic behavior remains in great flux. Because of the separate classifications of neurotic and psychotic behavior, we run into not only problems of interpretation, but also of clinical treatment issues. Where does one draw the line between visionary and psychotic? Can both labels be appropriate at the same time? To review again *Moi's* words: *"C'est un composé de hauteur et de bassesse, de bon sens et de déraison"*.[89]

The larger difference between *folie* and *déraison* is intentionality and even enjoyment in *folie*. *Le fou* becomes separated from society and is eventually objectified. Objectification occurs because there is a need to explain the function of such a *marginal* person, and the need to control and possess what is beyond control. James Creech explains the progression of objectification through his understanding of Foucault's *Les mots et les choses*:

> Unlike the previous episteme in which one made random and endless lists of things in the world, the new system of representation automatically involves "analysis" of which it represents. The inaugural moment representing identity between words and things leads to an ordering of these word things among themselves according to their characteristic differences from each other.[90]

Diderot advises the reader in the following passage that the nephew is abnormal. Yet we are led to believe that because of the nephew's frankness, he is closer to the truth than most.

> Lui. Moi, point du tout. Que le diable m'emporte si je sais au fond ce que je suis. En général, j'ai l'esprit rond comme une boule, et le caractère franc comme l'osier ; jamais faux, pour peu que j'ai intérêt d'être vrai ; jamais vrai pour peu que j'ai intérêt d'être faux.[91]

---

[89] Diderot, *Le Neveu*, 78.

[90] James Creech, *Diderot: Thresholds of Representation* (Columbus: Ohio University Press, 1986), 5.

[91] Diderot, *Le Neveu*, 132.

The truths expressed by the nephew might seem more palpable if we could label him insane. Truths told by seemingly normal people are harder to recognize because they are usually couched in terms society finds acceptable. The effect of naked truth is much too threatening. Selecting a crazy person to express the truth distances the individual from the individual and from society, rendering it more psychologically acceptable. Eccentricity is tolerable, or even justifiable, and deserving of public sympathy, and because the truth that is uttered by a "crazy," raving person can later be dismissed. These lines from *Le Neveu* describe how the nephew's unbridled tongue helps others to realize certain truths. S'il en paraît un dans une compagnie ; c'est un grain de levain qui fermente et qui restitue à chacun une portion de son individualité naturelle.[92]

The truth also serves to bring an individual closer to his/her inner being or a person's natural individuality. The truth the nephew espouses is made more palatable because we are programmed to deem him, rather than what he says, as unacceptable.

> Il secoue, il agite ; il fait approuver ou blâmer ; il fait sortir la vérité ; il fait connaître les gens de bien ; il démasque les coquins ; c'est alors que l'homme de bon sens écoute, et démêle son monde.[93]

As the discourse progresses in the novel it becomes increasingly complex. Soon after this passage, there is an intersection of worlds and a breach of psychological boundaries. The striated nature of the conversation reflects a fragmented individual. He is entertaining, yet curiously bizarre. The reader is made to feel uncomfortable with the actions of the nephew, such as the selling of his wife into prostitution. In this manner, reading *Le Neveu de Rameau* can be likened to experiencing the theatre of Bertolt Brecht, where the spectator becomes

---

[92] Diderot, *Le Neveu*, 72.

[93] Diderot, *Le Neveu*, 72.

progressively distanced from the play.[94] Once again the reader's attention is introduced to the alienation technique employed by Diderot. In the explanation below, Lester Crocker helps to explain how Diderot's form of argumentation produces this phenomenon:

> The psychological dimension is as inseparable from the argumentation as is the aesthetic. In fact, one may even venture to say that the specific arguments are entities in themselves. Each one bears the stamp of character and individual experience.[95]

The total experience of reading *Le Neveu de Rameau* requires engaging and disengaging with the character, his actions, and his dialectical conversation with *Moi*. When in the dimension of reading the alter-self, one is ever mindful of the clinical nature of Diderot's work[96]. In *Le Neveu de Rameau*, we can understand

---

[94] The Brechtian theory of alienation follows a dialectical format described by Brecht as a break from the pleasing type of theatre of the past. "And the catharsis of which Aristotle writes-cleansing by fear and pity, or from fear and pity-is a purification which is performed not only in a pleasurable way, but precisely for the purpose of pleasure." Berthold Brecht, "A Short Organum for the Theatre," in *Avant Garde Drama*, ed. Bernard Dukore and Daniel C. Gerould, (New York: Bantam, 1969). The central notion of the theatre of alienation challenges the cathartic or pleasurable effect of classical theatre (with resolution as the end product) stating that it inhibits humans capacity to intellectually process what is seen on stage, therefore limiting analytical thought about what one is viewing. As mentioned earlier, Diderot sought to create a different type of dialogue. He too, opposed a classical style and in so doing instituted a dialectical format comparable in modern terms to the theatre of Brecht.

[95] Crocker, *Chaotic*, 92.

[96] When speaking of the conceptual history of *marginality* in psychoanalysis and its relationship to literature, Lionel Trilling had this to say:

> We must, however, keep it in mind that only a relatively few years earlier in the nineteenth century it had not been at all remarkable to base one's scientific interests on the humanities. This earlier attitude is represented to us in a convenient and accurate way by the figure of Goethe. We all know what store Goethe set by his own scientific researches, and we know what part Goethe's famous essay on Nature played not only in the life of Freud but also in the tradition of the "philosophes" and the Encyclopedists, who were preponderantly men of letters: the science of the late seventeenth century and the eighteenth century moved on a tide of literary enthusiasm and literary formulation. Lionel Trilling, *Sincerity and Authenticity*, (Cambridge: Harvard University Press, 1972), 78.

who the philosopher is only in relationship to the nephew, and this understanding is what makes a discussion of *marginality* in this work so complex:

> Un tel décapage des identités apparentes—morales ou logiques—s'étaie d'un modèle biologique. La rhétorique polyphonique dans laquelle se déploie l'étrangeté de l'homme singulier, exceptionnel mais franc—la "franchise" remplace dans cette satire de Diderot toute apologie catonisante de la "vérité"-est la face visible d'une nature convulsive, spasmique, centrée sur le système nerveux qui découvrent que, les médecins de l'époque et que Diderot adopte.[97]

The nephew chooses to be crazy and to *marginalize* himself because this is what makes him *original*. Rameau's nephew chooses the life of an outsider, because in this way he will be recognized as different, special, and especially not ordinary. When the nephew asks : "Quel parti ? De se montrer, d'affecter la plus grande sécurité, de se conduire comme à l'ordinaire ?"[98] we recognize that he is trying to focus attention on his own grandiosity. The relationship of the observer to the sufferer is the focus of this dynamic, and in many ways parallel to the way we consider *Moi's* relationship to *Lui*.

Ultimately the nephew cannot be diagnosed. He must be regarded as a "deconstructed" construct. He is part of a triad: reader, philosopher, and nephew. He is a multi-faceted character used by the author to explore, teach and entertain. The nephew presents a portrait of someone who is personally chaotic and acts without power of reason (*déraisonnable*). Yet he is only "un peu en marge" and later serves as a mouthpiece and example for certain artistic and philosophical forms of expression. This chapter confirms the existence of yet another paradox; the deviant personality in the eighteenth century had a place in society and that place was located on the margin. This personality had a function within society as well: to act as a truth-telling mirror to society.

---

[97] Kristeva, *Etrangers*, 204.

[98] Diderot, *Le Neveu*, 155.

With an emphasis on the individual and estrangement from the self, the term *marginality* connotes both mental and cultural alienation. *Le Neveu de Rameau* is Diderot's clearest expression of his preoccupation with the subject of *self-imposed marginality*. Diderot presents this particular type of marginalization by using the example of splintered individual, in this piece the nephew who is portrayed as psychologically fragmented. He is the quintessential *marginal* being, and with this in-depth characterization, the text at times appears almost as a clinical analysis. With this type of evidence, Diderot leaves litle doubt as to his philosophical endeavor to define a particular type of *marginal* behavior.[99]

---

[99] The nephew is Diderot's ideal actor, as well as the Homme de génie as an ideal artist, who is so consumed by his role that he in fact becomes possessed by it. Often the nephew comes out of his trance-like state and notices the spectator as if for the first time. In this sense he represents the ideal artist as a marginalized figure who must alienate himself by becoming one with his creation, not unlike the tale of Pygmalion.

Chapter Three

Against Her Will:

Forced Marginality in *La Religieuse*

In order to understand the significance of marginalization in *La Religieuse*, it is necessary to examine Diderot's scientific study of *marginal* personalities which he developed and refined through the medium of artistic creation. Diderot's strong interest in the topic is evidenced by his having populated his books with a remarkable collection of *marginal* characters. As Robert Mauzi noted in his introduction to the Folio edition:

> Diderot est toujours pénétré d'invention, de chercher et de l'amour du bizarre : son gibier, ce n'est pas l'homme ordinaire, mais ces "originaux" que le réel atteste, et que pourtant l'artiste seul sait voir.[100]

It is in *La Religieuse,* more than in any other work, that Diderot integrated his two main proclivities, as the scientist and the artist worked in tandem to produce a portrait of a marginalized woman whose struggle took place prior to the French Revolution.[101] The portraits of female characters in *La Religieuse* are informed by the study of society from the perspective of a proto-sociologist. Furthermore, as this perspective highlights the issue of misogyny in eighteenth-century France, it is not accidental that the *marginal* characters in this book are all female.[102] First there is Suzanne Simonin, the powerless young woman who is sent off to a convent against her will. Next, there is Suzanne's natural mother who cannot nurture her

---

[100] See the excellent introduction of Mauzi to his edition of the work: Mauzi, "Préface". For the textual analysis I continue to refer to the Hermann edition of *La Religieuse*.

[101] Biological determinism and its influence on the concept *of* marginalization are part of Diderot's scientific analysis. In this chapter, I will concentrate on the literary aspects of Diderot's analysis. A detailed discussion of *biologically predetermined* marginalization in Diderot's work is found in the fourth and final chapter of this work.

[102] This is but one facet of *marginality* that the novel highlights. *Marginality* serves as the link between truth and genius in the attempt to examine *marginality*.

illegitimate offspring because of her shame and guilt. The list of disturbed and flawed female characters continues with the appearance of Mère de Moni, Suzanne's spiritual mentor, then the Sœur Sainte Christine, Suzanne's tormentor, and finally the lesbian Mother Superior of Arpajon.

In 1760, Diderot wrote his sole epistolary novel, *La Religieuse,* and by using graphic examples he explores the distinctive concept of *forced* marginalization. *La Religieuse* is different in many ways from other works in Diderot's œuvre, but it is his attentiveness to the process of marginalization which truly distinguishes it from all of his other endeavors. It is easy to think of reasons Diderot would have become interested in, and later even obsessed with, all things *marginal.* Those who were closest to him were forcibly marginalized. Along with the example of Rousseau, one does not have to look too far for more instances of marginalization in Diderot's own life. His sister Angélique, who was also his goddaughter, died tragically in a convent. Angélique had chosen to become a nun, but died at the age of twenty-eight after being deemed insane for many years. Diderot claimed her insanity was a result of the hard work she was made to perform in the convent. In *La Religieuse*, Diderot draws the reader into the dark world of the convent where there are enforced margins, against which the heroine struggles continually.

In *La Religieuse*, Suzanne Simonin is forced into many untenable situations and Diderot portrays her struggle to escape the life of the convent as the focus of his novel. He describes a stark example of the notion of physical alienation in *La Religieuse* when Suzanne Simonin is forced to live as a nun, cloistered and physically removed from society, deprived of all social liberty. The consequences for the individual in this case begin with physical alienation, but other forms of alienation are soon to follow. Therefore, the individual arrives at a *marginal* position in relation to the norm during the process of alienation.

It appears that Diderot uses the family as a microcosm for the larger society and this fact underscores Suzanne's sense of exteriority in relationship to her family. Suzanne's illegitimacy is the driving force for her marginalization and through her depiction Diderot worked to give his audience a portrait of *forced marginality*. It is the issue of authority that defines the boundaries that ultimately separate the *marginal* person from the norm. From the beginning it is evident that the authorities that control Suzanne's fate originate within the family, but the concept of authority expands to include the larger society and especially the Church. It is worthy of note that eventually all of these institutions contribute to Suzanne's marginalization.

In *La Religieuse* Diderot's study of *forced* marginalization begins with the concept of the family. Suzanne's birth is a mockery of family authority and its sense of order. She correctly suspects her parents of hiding a secret because of the way she is treated. Indeed, she is illegitimate and lives her life psychologically alienated from her surroundings. This type of alienation is key to the portrayal of Suzanne's self-concept for she is depicted as drawing strength from her self-knowledge. She is a character who always follows her instincts and from the first pages we see that it directs her to cast doubt on the legitimacy of her own birth:

> Peut-être mon père avait-il quelque incertitude sur ma naissance ; peut-être rappelais-je à ma mère une faute qu'elle avait commise, et l'ingratitude d'un homme qu'elle avait trop écouté ; que sais-je.[103]

Suzanne's suspicions are aroused in this example, and we learn how they are perceived through the actions of others, as observed and articulated by Suzanne herself. In this manner, Diderot communicates the family's reluctance to accept Suzanne as one of them. For the author, the family functions as a microcosm of society and from this perspective we soon see how Suzanne becomes ostracized from all social circles.

The heroine's battle for acceptance within her own family sets the tone of the novel. She is introduced to the reader in the midst of her struggle to return to

---

[103] Diderot, *La Religieuse*, 84.

her nuclear family. First the family hopes that Suzanne will somehow accept her lot in life and voluntarily remove herself from public view, and when she refuses to comply, the process of *forced* marginalization begins.

Suzanne's illegitimacy and her deprivation of maternal and paternal love lead the reader to sympathize with the heroine. Suzanne has no money, no lasting relationships, and all those who attempt to befriend her die, as Diderot chose to kill off anyone who could possibly change her destiny. What could be more illustrative of the utter impossibility of Suzanne's acceptance into a social circle and the ineluctable nature of her fate?[104]

The central character's exteriority in relationship to the law, combined with her self-concept, has a direct effect on her position in the family. She is depicted as trying at all times to examine herself within a family dynamic.[105] The reader is allowed to perceive this through Suzanne's suspicions and the descriptions of her self-perception.

The protagonist of this novel has no stable or defined position inside the family and is perceived as posing a serious threat to its structure. She is victimized and ostracized by her mother, sisters, and presumed "father." Her victimization is compounded by the sisters' fear that they will not receive their proper dowries if Suzanne should marry or become a recognized part of the family's financial and social structure. Because of this threat, Suzanne must always function as a satellite on the perimeter of the family. She is forced out of the family fold and is made to think that she must not dare try to re-enter after the truth of her birth is acknowledged. This dark analysis is confirmed by Suzanne's statement to her

---

[104] This tactic is employed so that the heroine remains completely marginalized. By the end of the first description the reader is completely drawn into the text. One could even say the novel has a paradoxical effect in this way; the more alienated the heroine becomes, the more the reader is drawn into the text because of the identification with Suzanne's painful struggle.

[105] The word "dynamic" here is used within a psychoanalytic context and pertains to the relationships within the family.

mother: "Je suis éloignée d'ajouter à vos peines de quelque nature qu'elles soient."[106]

Suzanne is the scapegoat of her family, particularly of her mother.[107] Diderot demonstrates clearly how Suzanne's mother sets her apart from her sisters: "Ma fille, vous n'avez rien, vous n'aurez jamais rien ; le peu que je puis faire pour vous je le dérobe à vos sœurs : voilà les suites d'une faiblesse."[108] Suzanne also plays the role of martyr by surrendering to her fate as a victim. It is at this point that she begins the process of forced alienation. It is through Suzanne's perception, or more accurately, Diderot's depiction of her feelings for her "father," that we perceive her position in relationship to her father and her family:

> Il me sembla que j'avais deux cœurs : je ne pouvais plus penser à ma mère sans m'attendrir, sans avoir envie de pleurer ; il n'était pas ainsi de M. Simonin. Il est sûr qu'un père inspire une sorte de sentiments qu'on n'a pour personne au monde que lui ; on ne sait pas cela sans s'être trouvée, comme moi, vis-à-vis d'un homme qui a porté longtemps et qui vient de perdre cet auguste caractère ; les autres l'ignorent toujours. Si je passais de sa présence à celle de ma mère, il me semble que j'étais *une autre*.[109]

It is through the description of Suzanne's feeling of being *une autre* that we first clearly see the issue of *marginality* in this story. By being *the other*, Suzanne embarks upon the journey of *forced* marginalization. Suzanne's suspicions about her legitimacy are finally confirmed, and she is formally made *the other*.[110]

While Suzanne is first rejected by her family, she is further marginalized by the norms of society, as defined by the law and the church. Suzanne's

---

[106] Diderot, *La Religieuse*, 108.

[107] The word scapegoat is used here in the biblical sense of taking on the sins of the others and being punished for them.

[108] Diderot, *La Religieuse*, 109–10.

[109] Diderot, *La Religieuse*, 113, (emphasis mine.)

[110] The term *other* is here used in the sense understood by Tzvetan Todorov: Il s'agit donc dans les deux cas d'un relativisme rattrapé à la dernière minute par un jugement de valeur (nous sommes mieux que les autres; les autres sont mieux que nous), mais où la définition des entités comparées, "nous" et "les autres," reste, elle, purement relative. Todorov, *Nous et les Autres*, 355.

self-recognition coincides with her physical rejection and marginalization. Because Mme Simonin is too ashamed to reveal the truth to Suzanne herself, Père Seraphin acts as a go-between who reveals the truth to Suzanne.[111] Mme Simonin is a sinful woman; therefore, it is Père Seraphin who assumes authority, "Il y a longtemps que j'ai exhorté pour la première fois Madame votre mère à vous révéler ce que vous allez apprendre..."[112] The priest finally reveals the truth to Suzanne: "Et c'est elle qui m'a chargé de vous annoncer que vous n'étiez pas la fille de M. Simonin."[113]

One wonders why, instead of simply stating, "Vous n'êtes pas la fille de M. Simonin," Diderot uses the past tense *étiez* in reference to Suzanne's relationship to her father. It seems, from use of this verb tense, that the idea of "never" becomes implicit here. M. Simonin never considered Suzanne to be his rightful daughter and thus never treated her as such.

This denial is evident from the following: "Peut-être mon père avait-il quelque incertitude sur ma naissance ; peut-être rappelais-je à ma mère une faute qu'elle avait commise ?"[114] Suzanne begins the process of *forced* marginalization at birth, unalterably alienated from her family due to her mother's misguided actions. Suzanne is illegitimate and physically distanced from her family of origin. Because of this she later becomes psychologically alienated from each family or cloister to which she is supposed to belong.

---

[111] In Hebrew the priest's name *Seraphin* designates a type of angel. The primary role of an angel is to act as a go-between or messenger. But considering the nature of his duty here, the biblical connotation could be considered ironic. His name is also *Père*, which sets the authoritative tone and reiterates the theme of father as authority.

[112] Diderot, *La Religieuse*, 105.

[113] Diderot, *La Religieuse*, 105.

[114] Diderot, *La Religieuse*, 84.

Gita May, in her article entitled, "Rousseau's Anti-Feminism Reconsidered," points out that women in the eighteenth century were largely enclosed within institutions:

> When one approaches the eighteenth century, one encounters the two main vexing problems facing the condition of womanhood: the angel-devil images and stereotypes already described in Simone de Beauvoir's *Second Sex* and the entrapment of women within prison-like places (the home, marriage, the convent).[115]

May continues to explain that the institutions of family and marriage or the convent are represented in the novel of the eighteenth century as the proper place for a young woman:

> That women under the Old Regime were imprisoned in one way or another since birth was an existential given, widely if covertly, recognized even then. No wonder, therefore, that the family, the convent, marriage, and even the exotic metaphor of the harem are so prevalent in the eighteenth-century novel as literary representations of the sequestered young woman.[116]

As May notes, Diderot is not alone in using the convent to portray the fate of women in eighteenth-century society. Most compelling is Diderot's choice to write about the process of entrapment within these institutions, and in this work specifically the forced sequestration of a young woman in the convent. Suzanne becomes emblematic of this role of women in society.

At the time Diderot wrote *La Religieuse*, the concept of the family was changing. This is reflected in Diderot's work where he demonstrates that the nuclear family is supposed to be one that forms tight bonds. This new family would

---

[115] Gita May, "Rousseau's Anti-Feminism Reconsidered," in *French Women and the Age of Enlightenment*, Samia Spencer (Bloomington: Indiana University Press, 1984), 309.

[116] Gita May, "Anti-Feminism," 309.

also be supposed to keep out certain undesirable elements, such as illegitimacy, and to protect the interests of those within its smaller, more immediate, framework.[117]

The themes of interiority and exteriority correlate directly to the concept of *forced* marginalization in *La Religieuse*. Individuals separated from society are outside the norm, whether or not by choice. In mid-eighteenth-century France the nuclear family in particular becomes the center of society, and therefore functions as a microcosm of the larger polity. Those who create the idea of the norm and those who follow it are part of society and therefore within this boundary. All others who do not follow the prescribed societal rules fall outside the margin, and, no matter how they arrive in this position, become *marginal*.

The ideas of entrapment and exclusion determine what is interior or exterior in relationship to a given institution. Interiority is represented by institutions in *La Religieuse*: the family, the cloister and society. Not to belong to any of these institutions is the essence of exteriority here. Even though Suzanne is within an institution that mimics the family dynamic she is forced to live her life outside of her real family, thus remaining an outsider to her family of origin for the rest of the novel.

A parallel psychoanalytic interpretation of the opening pages of this novel also exposes an underlying notion of *forced* marginalization. It is through the tension of interiority and exteriority and the conflict of their constant juxtaposition that the idea of actual boundaries comes into play. Significant interplay between the notions of interiority and exteriority in *La Religieuse* appears along with the creation of a psychological margin formed by the use of imagery. The concept of interiority is first suggested by Suzanne's coach ride home: [118]

---

[117] Traditional attitudes and family relationships to which I refer in this chapter generally date from the seventeenth century and persisted through most of the eighteenth century. This picture is drawn primarily from French society. For the socio-historical background is: Philippe Aries, *Centuries of Childhood* (New York: Vintage Random House, 1962), 339–64.

[118] These notions also demonstrate a strong presence of other literary tropes such as metaphor. The effect that the varying literary techniques, such as the juxtaposition of opposing

Je la suivis jusqu'à la porte conventuelle, là je montai dans une voiture où je trouvai ma mère seule qui m'attendait ; je m'assis sur le devant, et le carrosse partit. Nous restâmes l'une vis-à-vis de l'autre quelque temps sans mot dire ; j'avais les yeux baissés, je n'osais la regarder. Je ne sais pas ce qui se passa dans mon âme, mais tout à coup je me jetai à ses pieds et je penchai ma tête sur ses genoux ; je ne lui parlais pas, mais je sanglotais et j'étouffais. Elle me repoussa durement. Je ne me relevai pas ; le sang me vint au nez, je saisis une de ses mains, malgré qu'elle en eût, et l'arrosant de mes larmes et de mon sang qui coulait, appuyant ma bouche sur cette main je la baisais et je lui disais : Vous êtes toujours ma mère, je suis toujours votre enfant. . .[119]

This brief scene is replete with uterine and birth imagery. The first metaphor is womb-like and starts inside the coach: "Nous restâmes l'une vis-à-vis de l'autre." The separation begins after a birth-like push, "Elle me repoussa durement," and blood and other birth-like fluids appear: "et l'arrosant de mes larmes et de mon sang qui coulait". Next, Suzanne is made to spend six months in her room: "J'entrai dans ma nouvelle prison où je passai six mois sollicitant tous les jours inutilement la grâce de lui parler, de voir mon père ou de leur écrire."[120]

The shifting sense of interiority intensifies when Suzanne is finally granted an audience with her mother and by the description of her admission into the parlor. "C'était dans l'hiver. Elle était assise dans un fauteuil devant le feu ; elle avait le visage sévère, le regard fixe et les traits immobiles."[121]

This room functions as a symbol on two levels: the inside of a family and the inside of the mother's womb. The imagery comes to an abrupt halt when M.Simonin enters the room and says simply but forcefully, "Sortez", and thus the

---

images and the use of metaphor leave the reader to create the boundaries in his or her mind. These boundaries serve as limits for the heroine and they are used in almost every significant incident in the novel.

[119] Diderot, *La Religieuse*, 101–2.

[120] Diderot, *La Religieuse*, 102.

[121] Diderot, *La Religieuse*, 108.

room ceases to function as a symbol[122] With one word, Suzanne is commanded to leave both her mother's side and the actual room. This single utterance announces the moment of separation from the mother, like an infant abruptly leaving the womb. [123]

> Je me renfermai dans ma petite prison. Je rêvai à ce que ma mère m'avait dit. Je me jetai à genoux, je priai Dieu qu'il m'inspirât ; je priai longtemps, je demeurai le visage collé contre terre. [124]

The new boundary outside the family defines the sphere of exteriority where the heroine will be located for the duration of the discourse. This delineation represents a clear psychological marker for the reader as well; Suzanne is ostracized and her need for identification becomes the reader's own. This last description completes the psychological catharsis. Suzanne's rejection by her original family is concretized when she is forced to live in a convent. Thus Suzanne is physically exterior to the nuclear family. She is always depicted as separate from her family and her surroundings, no matter what the circumstances. The reader follows the course of *forced* marginalization as Suzanne is accepted by her first mother superior and then cruelly rejected by the next.

La Religieuse is divided into three different episodes, each of which is demarcated by the appearance of a new mother figure. The three mothers superior reflect aspects of Suzanne's birth mother and each exhibits a unique personality flaw. In the first episode, after Suzanne takes leave of her real family, she finds herself in new family conflict. Suzanne's birth mother is portrayed as unfeeling and unable to cope with her adulterous transgression, and thus incapable of fostering the natural mother-child bond. Mme de Moni, Suzanne's first mother

---

[122] Diderot, *La Religieuse*, 111.

[123] Later she is banished from the family forever: «Adieu Suzanne; ne demandez rien à vos , elles ne sont pas dans un état de vous secourir; n'espérez rien de votre père, il m'a précédé; il a vu le grand jour, il m'attend, ma présence sera moins terrible pour lui que la sienne pour moi.» Diderot, *La Religieuse*, 127.

[124] Diderot, *La Religieuse*, 111.

superior, and first maternal surrogate, is overcome by her own powerlessness in her relationship with Suzanne. Sœur Sainte-Christine is portrayed as a sado-masochist, and the Mother Superior of Arpajon presents one of the most notorious portraits of lesbianism in the eighteenth century. Her struggle to find a place within the family dynamic remains the same, but the actual dynamic or family make-up changes when she encounters this particular mother superior.

By placing her in a convent, Diderot makes an attempt to retrieve and redefine Suzanne's family. The destructiveness inherent in all Suzanne's family encounters is juxtaposed against her will to survive and serves as a main theme in this story. With nothing to look forward to in her life, Suzanne must make a decision: to accept being placed in a convent or to fight against what has been prescribed for her by her parents. Although this conflict marginalizes Suzanne further, it also serves to keep her sane. Eventually, it is not insanity that marginalizes Suzanne, but her adherence to truth and reason. Her extraordinary strength under duress, a quality that is to be admired, makes her an even more unusual candidate for *forced* marginalization.

Soon after this episode, Suzanne is driven off to Longchamp, where she encounters the first of the three mothers superior. The Mère de Moni introduces herself to Suzanne and quickly conducts what appears to be a musical audition, asking her to sit at the harpsichord and play.[125] One reason that Suzanne is accepted into this convent is because of her reputation for musical talent as described here by Arthur Wilson:

---

[125] At the time *La Religieuse* was written, Longchamp enjoyed a great reputation for its musical performances, as described by Arthur Wilson: "She [Suzanne] is able to establish the necessary contact with lawyers--not by any means an easy thing for nuns to do-- because the Abbaye de Lonchamp is so famous for its Easter music that a large audience from Paris is attracted there each year. The fact that Croismare would know this increases the verisimilitude of his narrative." Wilson, *The Testing Years (Repr. of 1957 Ed. Diderot: The Testing Years)*, 384–5.

He (Diderot) depicts Sister Suzanne as having one of the best voices in the convent, with the result that she is shown off a bit in the parlors, giving her an opportunity to become somewhat acquainted with the visiting public.[126]

This talent is repeatedly referred to and proves to be Suzanne's salvation from many a difficult situation. After her mini-recital, Suzanne is handed over to the Mère de Moni:"Ma mère me remit entre les mains de la supérieure, me donna la main à baiser et s'en retourna".[127] A psychological transference takes place here.[128]

Suzanne uses the same process to transfer the affections she once had for her mother to the mother superior. The new "mother" fulfills many of Suzanne's needs and longings. But we see evidence of the mother superior's hidden agenda when Suzanne declares: "Son dessein n'était pas de séduire mais certainement c'est ce qu'elle faisait..."[129] Suzanne at first appears an unwilling candidate for the convent, but with the calculated affection given her by the mother superior, she is quick to change her mind.

The kindness and nurturing of the Mère de Moni enable her to win Suzanne's confidence. Emotionally, she replaces Suzanne's birth mother, who has completely rejected her. However, this adoption can be viewed from another perspective; Suzanne is blatantly manipulated into complacency by the actions of the Mère de Moni: "Elle [Mère de Moni] me plaignit, me consola, me fit espérer un avenir plus doux"[130] Suzanne is thrust into this new family dynamic and into the

---

[126] Wilson, *The Testing Years (Repr. of 1957 Ed. Diderot: The Testing Years)*, 385.

[127] Diderot, *La Religieuse*, 115.

[128] Psychological transference is the redirection of feelings and desires, especially those unconsciously retained from childhood, toward a new object, usually a psychoanalyst conducting psychotherapy Jean Laplanche and J-B. Pontalis, *The Language of Psycho-Analysis* (New York: Norton, 1973), 455–62.

[129] Diderot, *La Religieuse*, 119.

[130] Diderot, *La Religieuse*, 118.

interiority offered by its symbolism: "Cependant le temps du postulant se passa, celui de prendre l'habit arriva et je le pris". [131]

The comfort of being an insider does not last long for Suzanne. Eventually, all of the Mère de Moni's efforts to bring Suzanne into the fold of the convent family backfire. The mother superior herself begins to be psychologically absorbed by Suzanne:

> Je ne sais, me dit-elle, ce qui se passe en moi, il me semble quand vous venez que Dieu se retire et que son esprit se taise ; c'est inutilement que je m'excite, que je cherche des idées, que je veux exalter mon âme, je me trouve une femme ordinaire et bornée ; je crains de parler...[132]

The idea of a thwarted psychological transference becomes relevant in this framework. Typically, a struggle to balance the relationship occurs in a psychodynamic relationship. Diderot's depiction of the psychodynamics of Suzanne's attachment to the Mère de Moni, though fictional, rings true. The mother-child relationship has left Suzanne so deprived of nurturing that it is impossible for her to refuse the attention showered upon her by the Mère de Moni. This mother superior also knows the human heart. She plays the perfect mother to her postulant children: "Allons, mon enfant, mettons-nous à genoux et prions..."[133] She is a mother figure in the psychological sense as well, as Diderot highlights the Mère de Moni's maternal instincts in this way:

> C'était une femme de sens qui connaissait le coeur humain ; elle avait de l'indulgence, quoique personne n'en eût moins besoin ; nous étions tous ses enfants.[134]

Soon afterward, when Suzanne enters the order, she exhibits more security in her new relationship. She recites her vows and passively accepts the veil in a

---

[131] Diderot, *La Religieuse*, 118.

[132] Diderot, *La Religieuse*, 119. (Ellipsis original.)

[133] Diderot, *La Religieuse*, 118.

[134] Diderot, *La Religieuse*, 117.

confused mental state. In a matter of fact manner she says, "Cependant le temps du postulat se passa, celui de prendre l'habit arriva et je le pris".[135] Suzanne is in a distracted mental state. This is confirmed by her inability to recollect any of the ceremony, as she will later confess to the Sœur Sainte-Christine: "J'étais si peu à moi, que je ne me rapelle pas même d'y avoir assisté".[136] Here Diderot describes Suzanne as existing in a state of psychological denial, and once again demonstrates his skill at probing the human psyche, pre-figuring Freud and modern psychology.[137]

Suzanne's emotional needs appear to be deep, and once the relationship with the Mère de Moni commences, she begins to exhibit what the modern reader would refer to as a psychological affect. Diderot had already identified these unfulfilled emotional needs in individuals deprived of childhood nurturing, by describing Suzanne's reactions in an extreme emotional state. Henceforth, Suzanne absorbs all the emotional support the mother superior has to offer:

> Ah ! Chère enfant, me dit-elle, qu'elle effet cruel vous avez opéré sur moi ! Voilà qui est fait, l'Esprit s'est retiré, je le sens ; allez, que Dieu vous parle lui-même, puisqu'il ne lui plaît pas de se faire entendre par ma bouche.[138]

Finally it is the Mère de Moni who will die. At the end of the episode, the Mère de Moni's death presents a striking tableau:

> A l'approche de sa mort, elle se fit habiller ; elle était étendue sur son lit ; on lui administra les derniers sacrements ; elle tenait un Christ entre ses bras. C'était la nuit : la lueur des flambeaux éclairait cette scène lugubre. Nous l'entourions, nous fondions en larmes, sa cellule retentissait des cris, lorsque tout à coup ses yeux brillèrent ; elle se releva brusquement, elle parla sa voix était presque aussi forte que dans l'état de santé ; le don qu'elle

---

[135] Diderot, *La Religieuse*, 118.

[136] Diderot, *La Religieuse*, 152.

[137] Scenes like these are reminiscent of the character of the nephew.

[138] Diderot, *La Religieuse*, 120.

avait perdu lui revint : elle nous reprocha des larmes qui semblaient lui envier un bonheur éternel.[139]

The scene is set: from the lighting to the atmosphere the painting is complete. As Jay Caplan points out, Diderot seems to have a deeper agenda for this tableau, and it is one in which the image of the family still holds a prominent place:

> Not only do these instances make the tableau, they also represent themselves. They are doubly the subject of the tableau, its maker and its topic just as the family relationships that the tableau represents are repeated in the relationship among the author, character and beholder.[140]

As summarized by Caplan, the description at the end of this episode serves the artistic purpose of closure, framing the narrative in the reader's mind as an end to a chapter. The Mère de Moni dies surrounded by her family, of which Suzanne is a part.[141]

It is striking that Diderot withholds a psychological description until after disclosing the mother superior's reasonable demeanor:

> C'était une Madame de Moni qui entrait en charge lorsque je fus conduite dans la maison. Je ne puis vous en dire trop de bien ; c'est pourtant sa bonté qui m'a perdue. C'était une femme de sens . . .[142]

Similar to Diderot's other female characters in this novel, the Mère de Moni is described from several vantage points. It is interesting to note that here that Diderot uses the word *sens* in the sense of *bon sens*. In the Age of Enlightenment

---

[139] Diderot, *La Religieuse*, 125.

[140] Jay Caplan, *Framed Narratives: Diderot's Genealogy of The Beholder* (Minneapolis: Minnesota University Press, 1985), 20.

[141] Almost as an afterthought Diderot then adds a paragraph in *La Religieuse* in the form of a letter from Suzanne's mother reporting the deaths of Suzanne's natural mother and "father." The letter reveals little about the circumstances of Mme Simonin's death and the lack of information given in this important transitional paragraph emphasizes the shallowness of Suzanne's familial relationships. Diderot, *La Religieuse*, 125.

[142] Diderot, *La Religieuse*, 116–7.

the quality of *bon sens* was highly regarded and Diderot himself thought it was a most important quality, and until the writing of *La Religieuse*, Diderot typically depicted it as a man's faculty.[143]

Suzanne, too, is accorded a certain respect for her intellect. Although the family milieu is destructive, it is also Suzanne's first exposure to legalistic reasoning: "J'en reconnais la justice."[144] With the help of a friend, Suzanne finally contacts a lawyer to represent her in court. This action demonstrates that Suzanne possesses a high level of reasoning, and it is probable that the example of her lawyer step-father influences her to have the case argued in court. [145] She reveals her knowledge of the law on the issue of rescinding her vows:

> Je ne suis plus surprise des distinctions qu'on a mises entre mes sœurs et moi, j'en reconnais la justice, j'y souscris ; mais je suis toujours votre enfant...[146]

Even though Suzanne tries to remain loyal to her mother, she has recourse to the legal system and assumes that on some level it must be just. This seems to be Diderot's set-up: to depict Suzanne in an environment where she is exposed to legalistic reasoning and then to have her use a legalistic approach for an attack on the system itself.

---

[143] This term is defined in depth in: Georges Benrekassa, *Le Concentrique et L'Excentrique: Marges Des Lumières* (Paris: Payot, 1980), 32.

[144] Diderot, *La Religieuse*, 109.

[145] Not many cases like this were actually argued before a magistrate in the mid-eighteenth century, which makes the argument put forth by Georges May that Marguerite Delamarre served as a model for the character of Suzanne Simonin all the more plausible. Georges May, "Diderot et La Religieuse" (New Haven: Yale University Press, 1954), 47. In 1990 I researched the written legal briefs of Joly de Fleury in the *Bibliothèque Nationale de Paris* for the years 1750-1760. The case of Marguerite Delamarre, though quite different from the story created by Diderot, is indeed the only one where a nun applies for release through a legal channel to try to leave the convent where she is forced to live. The actual manuscript also reports that Marguerite Delamarre was deemed *non-receivable*. (That is to say her request was denied.) She was made to remain in the convent where she eventually died some years later.

[146] Diderot, *La Religieuse*, 108.

Legal reasoning also serves to emphasize the idea of authority, especially male authority, in the novel. In her article "Happy Mothers and Other New Ideas in French Art," Carol Duncan elucidates this point:

> Fathers and husbands stood for authority, not companionship. Especially in bourgeois and peasant families, where paternal authority was absolute, the father was a severe figure. He ruled his wife — and her property — and decided the fates of his children with full legal sanction. Veneration and obedience, not love and affection, were his traditional due...[147]

The notion of *forced marginality* is based on the central concept of patriarchal authority, thus establishing its context at home, and within the family and by the father. In this description of Suzanne's adoptive father, Diderot calls attention to male, patriarchal and familial authority, and to the attempts to define societal margins:

> Mon père, homme d'un excellent jugement, mais homme pieux, était renommé dans sa province pour sa probité rigoureuse. Il fut, plus d'une fois, choisi pour arbitre entre ses concitoyens ; et des étrangers qu'il ne connaissait pas lui confièrent souvent l'exécution de leurs dernières volontés.[148]

Diderot approaches the issue of patriarchal authority systematically, as we see in *L'Entretien d'un père avec ses enfants*, where he discusses authority and defines psychological boundaries, beginning at the level of the smallest unit, the family, and moving out to the larger society.[149] As Wilson observes:

> The discussion gave the author an opportunity to describe the compassionate but evenhanded justice of the father, the generous and tender impulses of his sister, the harsh and unbending qualities of his *abbé* brother, and his own magnanimous and somewhat quixotic impulses. Although

---

[147] Carol Duncan, "Happy Mothers and Other New Ideas in French Art," *The Art Bulletin*, December 1973, 573.

[148] Denis Diderot, *L'Entretien d'un père avec ses enfants*, eds Herbert Dieckmann and Jean Varloot, Œuvres Complètes (Paris: Hermann, 1989), 89.

[149] Wilson, *Diderot*, 219.

written much later, it must surely describe the family group of this very time.[150]

Here Diderot clearly underlines the father's attributes that make him authoritative. He depicts the father in the *Entretien* as a man of great judgment, even if he is pious. For example, the almost sarcastic use of the conjunction *mais,* which could translate as "even if" in the passage above, demonstrates Diderot's hostility to the Church. In Diderot's estimation authority functioned on different levels. The first level would be the family structure and the second level would be the society and the state. Both institutions derive greater definition from the authoritative realm of the Church.[151]

In *La Religieuse*, the father is not only depicted as the authority figure of the family, but as an authority in the social and the legal sphere. He is the one who sets the law and uses it to demarcate the boundaries of society. One could say that Diderot uses the father to define the family structure, while he uses the lawyer to define the structure of society at large. It is significant that in *La Religieuse*, Mme Simonin is not condemned for forcing her daughter out of the home, and in addition, only the father's legal rights are mentioned: ". . . Il ne doute point que vous ne lui apparteniez comme enfant que par la loi qui les attribue à celui qui porte le titre

---

[150] Wilson, *Diderot*, 217.

[151] Diderot's *Lettre sur les Aveugles* and his subsequent imprisonment in Vincennes demonstrate his negative attitude toward the authorities of Church and State. Diderot protested that enlightened people should not be forced to believe ideas upon the authority of Church and State, but that observation and experimentation yielded solid truths:

> Des personnages de la première distinction ont eu l'honneur de partager son refus avec les philosophes; en un mot, il n'a voulu laisser tomber le voile que devant quelques yeux et sans conséquence. Si vous êtes curieuse de savoir pourquoi cet habile académicien fait si secrètement des expériences qui ne peuvent avoir, selon vous, un trop grand nombre de témoins éclaires, je vous répondrai que les observations d'un homme aussi célèbre ont moins besoin de spectateurs quand elles se font, que les auditeurs, quand elles sont faites. Denis Diderot, *Lettres sur les aveugles*, ed. Robert Nicklaus, Œuvres Complètes (Paris: Hermann, 1978), 25.

d'époux."[152] Again Diderot highlights the importance of the "law" as the principle defining the society and setting the family boundaries.

The establishment of patriarchal authority, and consequentially its limitations, begins at a very early stage in the novel. The second paragraph of *La Religieuse* commences with these words: "Mon père était avocat".[153] These few words have a profound effect on the shaping of the notion of *marginality*: *père* is the authority figure of the family in a patriarchal society. The *avocat* or lawyer is one who interprets and ultimately manipulates the law, lending definition to what marks out the limits of society. By definition, the father figure, also coincidentally a lawyer by profession indicates who is *marginal*.

Here, as in any patriarchal society, authority originates from the father and is passed to the son. As there are no sons in this family, the two older daughters stand to inherit the family's assets. However, the daughters' authority is mediated through their husbands as they hold the ultimate power over their wives' inheritance. Therefore, Suzanne's brothers-in-law *inherit* authority and ensure that Suzanne's deprivation and exclusion is complete. Suzanne is not entitled to an inheritance and of course, has no one to advocate for her. She realizes the extent to which she is financially deprived, but is more affected by the facts that she has no father, and that her mother cannot be nurturing. Furthermore, all traces of her biological father have been erased, so she has no possible legal claim on her "father."

> Je n'avais point de père ; le scrupule m'avait ôté ma mère ; des précautions prises pour que je ne pusse prétendre aux droits de ma naissance légale ; une captivité domestique fort dure ; nulle espérance, nulle ressource.[154]

---

[152] Diderot, *La Religieuse*, 107.

[153] Diderot, *La Religieuse*, 82.

[154] Diderot, *La Religieuse*, 107.

The male figures in *La Religieuse* are either fathers, priests, (addressed as "father,") or lawyers, and these three male roles form a conceptual triangle, thus denoting a trinity of authority (family, church, and nation) and a furthering of the religious symbolism. All of the male figures serve important authoritative functions; they involve themselves with setting the limits of society. From this portrait, it is clear that the author does not envision women fulfilling these authoritative functions. The rules and laws presented by these authority figures serve as boundaries that the non-authority characters are to follow strictly.

The literature and visual arts of mid-eighteenth-century France are replete with signs that the aristocracy and the bourgeoisie were questioning religion in all of its aspects, including theological and institutional. For example, Diderot wrote abundantly and fervently in his *Salons* about the paintings of Jean-Baptiste Greuze, whose paintings underscore the theme of *marginality* and date from approximately the same period that Diderot wrote *La Religieuse*. Diderot's choice of works to treat in his *Salons* especially reflected this ferment. One painting in particular, *La dame de charité*, by Greuze, epitomizes the marginalization of the Church and highlights the rationale for the choice of nun as a *marginal* character. This painting depicts a patriarchal figure on his death-bed, with his family in the background. A charitable woman is in the foreground, showing her daughter how to care for the infirm elderly man. The figure of a nun is evident in the back right corner of the painting. She is painted in obscuring shades and is clearly in a *marginal* position in the painting. This painting speaks to the mentality of the time. Diderot was himself in the middle of a pronounced anti-ecclesiastical phase at the time of this novel's inception. Thus his choice of a sacred setting for the novel *La Religieuse* is most fitting to his purpose. He sets the tone in a passage where he offers one of his most damning portraits of cloistered life and of the Church in general:

> Ces femmes se vengent bien de l'ennui que vous leur portez ; car il ne faut pas croire qu'elles s'amusent du rôle hypocrite qu'elles jouent, et des

sottises qu'elles sont forcées de vous répéter : cela devient à la fin si usé et si maussade pour elles...[155]

Here in this episode, Suzanne serves as a mouthpiece for the author, who not only condemns the church but describes the entire cloistered lifestyle as *marginal*. Not only is it *marginal*, but for Diderot it is beyond the pale of decency:

Car il est sûr, Monsieur, que, sur cent religieuses qui meurent avant cinquante ans, il y en a cent tout juste de damnées, sans compter celles qui deviennent folles, stupides, ou furieuses en attendant.[156]

In the next section, Suzanne's non-conformity is her undoing. As mentioned previously, the transition from one episode to the next is abrupt. Yet the nature of the actions in the next episode, act as a warning to the reader, for they serve as an introduction to the next emotional stage of the book. Not only does the depiction of evil in the convent taint the institution of religion, but it also serves to parody the family structure which is depicted as a perverse model for cloistered life.

In *La Religieuse* the religious theme thus replicates the idea of a family dynamic as Diderot attempts to re-establish the design of the nuclear family. The clearest proof of this is in the names chosen by the Church for its various members: *father, mother superior, sisters, brothers*, etc. In fact, Suzanne is surrounded only by *sisters* as she was in her former family. The familial and religious imagery interact once again within the walls of the convent. As Diderot shows the inherent cruelty of both institutions, his depictions serve to deepen the sense of entrapment and interiority in the novel.

Through his critical portrayal of the Church in *La Religieuse*, Diderot challenges the role of institutional authority.[157] The family, the patriarchal society

---

[155] Diderot, *La Religieuse*, 92.

[156] Diderot, *La Religieuse*, 92.

[157] Arthur Wilson reveals that Diderot had first-hand knowledge of the machinations of both the Church and government: The French Enlightenment did not merely originate new ideas: it

including the legal system, and the Church are all introduced in authoritative forms. The appearance of three institutions once again presents the idea of a triangle, which could even suggest the Christian Trinity. With the repetition and insistence on this image, Diderot uses religious imagery to critique the very institution that generates it and which he views so negatively.

Diderot uses Suzanne's social rejection not only to describe the familial, religious and societal boundaries of her world, but also to unmask the hypocrisy within French society at the time in regard to the prevalence of adulterous affairs in this stratum of French society. These affairs were tacitly condoned as a part of the marriage agreement. Blandine McLaughlin offers a frank picture of the mores of the times:

> The majority of the time, husband and wife lived separate lives, once descendants were provided; and so long as outward appearances were maintained, each arranged his sentimental life as he saw fit, without objection from either partner.[158]

Nevertheless, devout Catholics aspired to maintain, at the least, the appearance of adhering to traditional values and beliefs. However, as stated earlier, adultery was certainly not considered acceptable by the Church. Mme Simonin is depicted as a practicing Catholic and is culpable because she could not simply confess her sin and wash it away. Her sexual transgression taints her for the remainder of her life. She is constantly reminded of her sin when Suzanne is present. This perceived state of unatoneable sin is repeated throughout the novel, not only to highlight the contradiction in Suzanne's *marginality*, but also to define and even to mock the margins of society as Diderot saw them. According to Diderot, the Church is a cruel institution that promotes a child's rejection from its family.

---

applied them to existing institutions. Wilson, *The Testing Years (Repr. of 1957 Ed. Diderot: The Testing Years)*, 92.

[156] Blandine McLaughlin, "Diderot and Women," in *French Women and the Age of Enlightenment*, Samia Spencer (Bloomington: Indiana University Press, 1984), 302.

Suzanne suspects her mother of having committed adultery from the outset of the novel. As she questions her origin she also challenges prevailing authority. Her actions suggest the often conflicting "intelligent *naiveté*" that forms part of her personality. Ever mindful of her situation, she demonstrates her knowledge of what was considered proper behavior for a woman in French eighteenth-century society. "Je me conduisis avec discrétion. Je crus pouvoir répondre de moi".[159]

Suzanne is born illegitimate into a milieu where extra-marital affairs are frequent and children from these unions often hold questionable positions in society. Society often tolerated "natural children" while the Church rejected the very notion.[160] Suzanne's illegitimacy is pitted against her desire to belong. Diderot uses this formula to begin a negative pattern that keeps the heroine constantly threatened. In so doing, Diderot shows evidence that he understands complex psychological defense mechanisms.

Diderot's depiction of Suzanne demonstrates that through stress and repeated trauma, psychological defenses often become weakened. He also demonstrates a nascent understanding of complex psychoanalytic concepts. For example, Suzanne is threatened numerous times, and Diderot depicts her psychological reactions to these stresses in a careful and scientific manner. For the most part these depictions seem very realistic except perhaps for the remarkable extent to which Suzanne is able to persevere. Suzanne is described as having exceptional powers of reason, and through almost all of the hardship that assaults her mental state, she remains surprisingly stable. Her ability to muster such psychological strength in the face of adversity gives Suzanne an almost

---

[159] Diderot, *La Religieuse*, 97.

[160] This phenomenon is highlighted by Carol Duncan who notes that: "So called 'natural children' were produced in abundance and often acknowledged at all levels of society." Duncan, "Happy Mothers," 572.

superhuman quality. Ultimately, she adheres to her power of reason, which is what preserves her sanity.[161]

According to Diderot, reason is a man's way of thinking: a woman thinks with another part of her anatomy: the womb. In *Sur les femmes*, for example, women are depicted as being governed by their hormonal constitution rather than by their minds, while men are rational and reasonable beings governed by their intellect:

> La femme porte au-dedans d'elle-même un organe susceptible de spasmes terribles, disposant d'elle et suscitant dans son imagination des fantômes de toute espèce. C'est dans le délire hystérique qu'elle revient sur le passé, qu'elle s'élance dans l'avenir, que tous les temps lui sont présents. C'est de l'organe propre à son sexe que partent toutes ses idées hystériques.[162]

Yet we see in *La Religieuse* that Suzanne uses a man's power of reason, for if reason defined the law and most men were reasonable, they would act within the margins of a self-defined society.

In this novel Diderot advocates the power of reason contrasted against the cold rationalism represented by Suzanne's "father."[163] M. Simonin is a rational being and he is also a cold and often cruel character. Père Séraphin, her mother's confessor, reports only the bare truth and rational options to Suzanne, never once exhibiting consideration for her state of mind. Finally, M. Manouri, Suzanne's

---

[161] This point is especially important in the context of the eighteenth century where the "superhuman" woman becomes the precursor to the romantic ideal.

[162] Denis Diderot, *Sur les femmes,* ed. Elizabeth Badinter (Paris: Plon, 1989), 41.

[163] Diderot's *rationalism* is the faculty of thinking logically, and is divorced from intuition and emotion. Reason is a manner of comprehending or making inferences which includes an analytical way of thinking, but can be linked to the emotions if they are moderate. Numerous male characters are typically depicted as truly *rational* beings, and many are also reasonable. According to Diderot women are often almost "hysterical" and therefore cannot truly exhibit either faculty. In the estimation of Michel Foucault, Foucault, *Histoire de la Folie à l'âge classique*, 397–8, the Marquis de Sade followed a "rational" course of thought. This distinction is developed in greater detail in an article by Stockinger who gives an accounting of the importance of the differentiation between reason and rationalism in the French eighteenth-century context: Stockinger, "Homosexuality in the French Enlightenment".

lawyer, underestimates the power of reason, and Diderot points this out in M. Manouri's first attempt to defend Suzanne:

> M. Manouri publia un premier mémoire qui fit peu de sensation ; il y avait trop d'esprit, pas assez de pathétique, presque point de raisons.[164]

Unfortunately for Suzanne, the *mémoire* published by M. Manouri was not as powerful as it might have been had he relied on his ability to reason.

Suzanne's mood changes steadily from the beginning of the second episode, from defiance to despair. At this time, Suzanne has to face the threatening situation of physical danger. Suzanne then becomes an outcast from her own small group of nuns, as they too succumb to the pressure of the new mother superior.[165] The only one to remain loyal is the Sœur Ste. Ursule who puts Suzanne in contact with her lawyer.

Being a favorite postulant of the Mère de Moni had set Suzanne apart from the other nuns. Though she had been separated from the others when she had been spending time with the Mère de Moni, she was considered better, and therefore treated with greater respect and at times even regarded with awe. But Suzanne is abruptly displaced in this episode from her privileged position as favorite to that of the most despised sister. It is no exaggeration to see a religious parallel here: Suzanne's rejection is a fall from grace.

The second episode portrays Suzanne's persecution and degradation. The first picture in this particular section is that of a mother superior who institutes her repressive regime from the moment she enters the convent:

> La seconde, au contraire, renvoya à chaque religieuse son cilice et sa discipline, et fit retirer le Nouveau et l'Ancien Testament.[166]

Here, in the continuation of the passage, the new order is depicted in all its rigidity:

---

[164] Diderot, *La Religieuse*, 181.

[165] This idea of rejecting the rejected is also seen in Diderot's *Le Neveu de Rameau*, in the passage where he relates the story of the "Fou de Bertin."

[166] Diderot, *La Religieuse*, 130.

> L'autorité des maîtresses se trouva très bornée ; elles ne pouvaient plus disposer de nous comme leurs esclaves.[167]

Significantly, Diderot uses terms that imply existing limitations like *bornée*, thus establishing an underlying tone of structure and authority within the text.

In the convent, Suzanne wears an amulet around her neck that was given to her by the Mère de Moni, and she deeply cherishes this gift. In context, the meaning of her wearing of the ritual ornament can be looked upon as a religious metaphor. This necklace is worn instead of her crucifix. The Mother Superior of Moni (the Mère de Moni) in her martyrdom now becomes a surrogate for Jesus. Suzanne, who is a victim and martyr herself, identifies with the mother superior and her suffering. It is as if she herself were suffering for the sins of Suzanne, (and perhaps for Suzanne's real mother, too). The mother superior does, in fact, assume a Christ-like role in her relationship with Suzanne.[168] The Mère de Moni becomes increasingly absorbed by Suzanne and is slowly being abandoned by God for reasons beyond her control. Suzanne thus assumes a central place in the Mère de Moni's life.

In his exploration of *marginality* Diderot exhibits an acute clinical awareness. Other aspects of Diderot's explanation of *marginal* social roles appear in his novel *La Religieuse,* most notably in the character of the Mère Supérieure d'Arpajon, who presents an interesting combination of *marginal* characteristics. We see here many instances of *forced* marginalization in the novel *La Religieuse* and here Diderot showcases yet another type of *marginality*. This type of marginalization is biological in origin, where characters are depicted with some type of organic deformity that, in the context, necessitates their alienation from society. This form of *marginality* is imposed by society's reaction to the impaired

---

[167] Diderot, *La Religieuse*, 130.

[168] The fact that she is incorporated as a religious symbol supports the thesis that Diderot was also meant to address marginalization in terms of the Church as an institution.

individual. In accordance with eighteenth-century attitudes, the Mère Supérieure is depicted as a sexual deviant; this is to say her homosexual personality is presented as unbalanced. As a lesbian within the context of convent life, the Mère Supérieure d'Arpajon is doubly outcast from the society at large and from a smaller, already marginalized group. The Mère Supérieure d'Arpajon becomes insane at the end of this story as well, driven out of her mind by her unrequited lust and love for Suzanne. Diderot prepares to lead the reader on a path to marginalization with the following vivid description: [169]

> Cette supérieure s'appelle madame...Je ne saurais me refuser à l'envie de vous la peindre avant d'aller plus loin. C'est une petite femme toute ronde, cependant prompte et vive dans ces mouvements. Sa tête n'est jamais assise sur ses épaules ; il y a toujours quelque chose qui cloche dans son vêtement ; sa figure est plutôt bien que mal ; ses yeux dont l'un, c'est le droit, est plus haut et plus grand que l'autre, sont pleins de feu et distraits ; quand elle marche elle jette ses bras en avant et en arrière ; veut-elle parler, elle ouvre la bouche avant que d'avoir arrangé ses idées, aussi bégaye-t-elle un peu ; est-elle assise, elle s'agite sur son fauteuil comme si quelque chose l'incommodait.[170]

The narrator is insistent on describing this character in detail and from this opening passage paints a colorful portrait of the Mother Superior from Arpajon. The Mother Superior from Arpajon speaks without thinking, and her unraveled discourse will produce truths that derive from the raw chaotic state of her ideas. The description of the mother superior's distracted eyes gives the first indication of a nervous personality and it becomes increasingly apparent that all is not quite right here. Diderot portrays this mother superior as significantly different from the rest and the above description is meant to cause discomfort and distance. Like

---

[169] The emphasis provides an analytic focus on the process of *becoming marginal* that appears at times to be even more important than the *marginal* person him/herself. This study of *process* gives us an insight into some of the first attempts at what could be considered a modern psychoanalytic perspective.

[170] Denis Diderot, *La Religieuse*, ed. Georges May, Œuvres Complètes (Paris: Hermann, 1975), 207–8.

Rameau's nephew, the lesbian mother superior is depicted as a person alienated from herself. In the process of his two-page description of this character Diderot demonstrates a type of disorder in her psychological and constitutional make-up. The word *décousu* here indicates the unraveling of the mother superior's soul and spirit. The psychological disentangling of the mother superior takes place on many levels and the disorder caused in the convent is due to its leader's psychological and physical unhinging. The body /mind connection of which Diderot speaks in the *Pensées sur l'interprétation de la nature* is once again emphasized in *La Religieuse*. *Ame* connotes both mind and body, for it is that combination that makes the soul, and the word *décousu* refers to *son esprit*. The disorder within her being is then related to the disordered regime in the convent.

> Sa figure décomposée marque tout le décousu de son esprit et toute l'inégalité de son caractère ; aussi l'ordre et le désordre se succèdent-ils dans la maison.[171]

In this passage Diderot quickly returns to "*sa figure*" and her physical description:

> Sa figure est plutôt bien que mal ; ses yeux, dont l'un, c'est le droit, est plus haut et plus grand que l'autre sont pleins de feu et distraits : quand elle marche elle jette ses bras en avant et en arrière.[172]

The Mother Superior of Arpajon fails to make eye contact and is intensely abrupt in her range of movements; her composite personality is depicted beyond the range of normal behaviors. There is disorder in her physical being, her personality, and externally, in her convent. In this one character Diderot melds and showcases all three types of *marginality*.

> Veut-elle parler ? Elle ouvre la bouche, avant que d'avoir arrangé ses idées ; aussi bégaye-t-telle un peu. Est-elle assise ? Elle s'agite sur son fauteuil, comme si quelque chose l'incommodait.[173]

---

[171] Diderot, *La Religieuse*, 208.

[172] Diderot, *La Religieuse*, 208.

[173] Diderot, *La Religieuse*, 208.

Here Diderot paints a portrait of an individual who seems alienated from herself because of a psychic rupture.[174] Within this description we see what Julia Kristeva refers to as a case of the self being inhabited by the other and the other being inhabited by the self.[175] The portrait of something that is *other* brings forth one of the many two-sided dialectics inherent in the work of Diderot, presented here within the biological make-up of his characters, reflected in dialogue and language. Both Rameau's nephew and the Mother Superior of Arpajon present types of "the two-sided conflicted personality."

As noted above, the alienation portrayed in this novel is of a double nature. The convent represents a group of women separated from society by their religious status and vows of chastity and poverty. The option to live a cloistered life is notionally a matter of choice, though sometimes this choice would be mandated because of economic disparity or other pressures for women were often left with no other options. It is an idealized view that the convent life is a freely chosen path to take vows and live a life separated from the more secular world. Diderot exposes the fallacy in this assumption by representing the crazy, lesbian mother superior as a *marginal* being separated from society by physical attributes, social behavior and sexual preference.[176]

Suzanne, having been pursued by the Mother Superior of Arpajon, does not reject the homosexual advances, but appears to be in denial, apparently unaware of what the mother superior intends. Diderot makes the reader question whether Suzanne is even cognizant of the fact that this is not the norm. As the psychological *anagnorisis* necessary for Suzanne to begin to change her situation has not yet

---

[174] I have referred to this behavior before in terms of a bipolar personality.

[175] This idea is discussed at length by Julia Kristeva in reference to *Le Neveu*. See: Julia Kristeva, *Desire in Language*, Leon Roudiez (New York: Columbia University Press, 1980).

[176] *Mme de la Carlière, Sur les Femmes*, and *Ceci n'est pas un conte,* are further examples of the marginalization of women in Diderot's works. These are included in the volume: Denis Diderot, *Oeuvres Complètes,* in *Vol. XII, Supplément au Voyages de Bougainville*, Dieckmann, Herbert (Paris: Hermann, 1989).

taken place, Suzanne is seemingly caught at a dead-end, and this fact justifies her response to the mother superior and her sexual advances. Suzanne is not only on the margin but is now stepping over the edge.

Diderot obliquely raises a number of questions about this particular type of *marginality* within his description of the lesbian mother superior. What is the basis for her specific homosexual behavior? Does she exert an influence on the other nuns in this respect? Is homosexuality treated as an environmentally imposed form of sexual expression, or is there an innate proclivity toward sexual orientation and behavior?

It seems that Diderot presents a view that homosexuality is environmentally imposed, yet there is room for an alternative but not mutually exclusive interpretation. If one considers Diderot's concept of biological determinism and applies it to this work, there is an indication that Diderot explores the possibility of a biological basis for homosexuality.

Diderot also expresses confusion, and from a modern perspective, misplaced or even false assumptions about different sexual behaviors. For example, in this episode he explores what will be later characterized as sado-masochism in practically the same breath as homosexuality. He uses these examples to demonstrate the chaos of Suzanne's life:

> Une religieuse, alors manque-t-elle à la moindre chose ? Elle la fait venir dans sa cellule, la traite avec dureté, lui ordonne de se déshabiller et de se donner vingt coups de discipline ; la religieuse obéit, se déshabille, prend sa discipline et se macère, mais à peine s'est-elle donné quelques coups, que la supérieure devenue compatissante, lui arrache l'instrument de pénitence, se met à pleurer ; qu'elle est bien malheureuse d'avoir à punir ![177]

Here the depictions of sado-masochism contribute to another psychological *anagnorisis* or recognition brought on by the imagination of physical pain. The shock of this pain is Suzanne's turning point. All of Suzanne's encounters with her

---

[177] Denis Diderot, *La Religieuse*, ed. Georges May, Oeuvres Complètes (Paris: Hermann, 1975), 209.

peers and superiors are painful, yet she overcomes them. The addition of physical violence from her second mother superior makes the situation untenable. The appearance of homosexuality is pivotal in this particular context, but it is the implicit violence in the mother superior's wish to dominate Suzanne by means of seduction that highlights the issue of *forced* marginalization in this novel. The mother superior in question is made to confess her sins and although she eventually dies insane, her confession both diminishes her guilt and justifies her behavior toward Suzanne. [178]

The inclusion of a lesbian character adds a new and profoundly affective dimension to the overall impression of *marginality* in this book. Diderot paints an unflattering portrait of the mother superior. Therefore, in light of the other disturbances presented in the depiction of her character, one could postulate that Diderot drew attention to homosexuality in order to call it into question. In his probing of the basis of homosexuality, the author leaves the impression that homosexuality is a behavior reflective of a pathological personality.

Because this book is an epistolary novel, we are ever aware of Suzanne's voice and therefore of her perspective. Her descriptions are marked by the subjectivity of her experiences. In the descriptions of the Sœur Sainte-Christine, the reader immediately senses that this mother superior is quite different from the Mère de Moni: "C'est la Sœur Sainte-Christine qui succéda à la Mère de Moni".[179] The Sœur Sainte-Christine is never referred to as "Mother," even from the first mention of her name. The appellation "sœur" for the new superior already intimates a demotion in status, because most mothers superior are referred to as *Madame* or

---

[178] Diderot also adds an insightful twist to this transition in the novel and suggests a kind of identification with the aggressor. It appears odd that the violence Suzanne experiences has less impact when recounted to the Church superiors than the homosexual advances of her last mother superior.

[179] Diderot, *La Religieuse*, 128.

Mère. The tension created by a change in forms of address reflects a change of status, although technically the mothers superior are of the same rank.

Motivated by her refined sense of justice, Suzanne refuses to accept the new authority, a stance that yields unpleasant consequences. Here, as earlier, the initial definition of boundaries is set by the presence of authority. Sœur Sainte-Christine tries from the moment of her arrival at Longchamp to establish her authority and sharply to curtail personal autonomy. In her severe asceticism, she institutes the use of the hair-shirt, the whip and the mixing of food with ashes. She orders the Bibles be removed from the sisters' bedrooms, thus replacing the familiar symbols of religious authority with her own extreme form and thus emphasizing the authority of the Church over the individual. It becomes apparent that Sœur Sainte-Christine is not only trying to alienate Suzanne but that she is pursuing a more intricate and despicable agenda: "Il m'est impossible d'entrer dans tout le petit détail de ses méchancetés ; on m'empêchait de dormir, de veiller, de prier".[180] Suzanne soon begins to exhibit signs of physical deterioration: "Ma santé ne tint point à des épreuves si longues et si dures je tombai dans l'abattement, le chagrin et la mélancolie".[181] Signs of mental unraveling and despair are soon to follow:

> Je me portais mes mains à ma gorge, je déchirai mes vêtements avec mes dents ; je poussai des cris affreux, je hurlai comme une bête féroce.[182]

In the first episode, while Suzanne is not yet physically mistreated, she is manipulated and spiritually seduced. In the second episode she is a victim of actual physical abuse. Her revulsion to convent life reappears only with the actual physical threat. Her strong reaction to persecution reflects Diderot's wish to portray her as a stalwart, yet human, character. "J'ai du courage, mais il n'en est

---

[180] Diderot, *La Religieuse*, 132.

[181] Diderot, *La Religieuse*, 132.

[182] Diderot, *La Religieuse*, 140.

point qui tienne contre l'abandon, la solitude et la persécution".[183] On the one hand, the pressure of physical victimization and of emotional and mental torture will eventually weaken her, but for the time that Sœur Sainte-Christine rules as superior, it is also her source of strength. We see confirmation of this in the lines which Suzanne utters when she reaches the limit of physical endurance: "En vérité je ne vivais que parce qu'elles souhaitaient ma mort".[184] She finally contemplates suicide, and in so doing, her actions help demonstrate Diderot's contempt for the Church, as the convent is also a metaphor for society, and here once again, the religious setting helped Diderot trace a course of marginalization.

The parallels to religious doctrine remain constant, yet the symbols of religion are mixed and even reversed at times. Suzanne, like Jesus, is not believed at first. Suzanne, like Jesus, develops a following; both are rejected, persecuted and become martyrs. Suzanne is made to assume the positions that Jesus is described as having adopted when he was himself victimized by his persecutors: "Elle (Suzanne) se compare à Jesus-Christ, et elle nous compare aux juifs qui l'ont crucifié".[185]

The view that Christianity itself is Suzanne's persecutor is also a valid interpretation. It is the religion of Christ that rules her life and the messengers of Christ carry out the punishment. Even the name Sœur Sainte-Christine reflects the author's deliberate attempt to connect Christianity and persecution in the episode of "Sainte-Christine." The name itself name ironically identifies the Christian religion as the oppressor. [186]

---

[183] Diderot, *La Religieuse*, 142.

[184] Diderot, *La Religieuse*, 134.

[185] Diderot, *La Religieuse*, 141.

[186]The choice of the name Suzanne is significant. The name Suzanne calls to mind the story of Susanna and the Elders in the Apocrypha. Susanna is the victim of false accusations of adultery after having refused improper advances of two lecherous elders who had been spying on her while she bathed. They threatened to blackmail her, if she would not have sex with them. The elders then follow through with their threat to accuse her of adultery, and she is to be put to death. However, a young man by the name of Daniel comes forward to defend Susanna, revealing discrepancies in the stories of the two accusers. The pair are executed in Susanna's stead. Like her

In the second episode Suzanne is depicted as physically alienated. The reader is now repositioned at the other end of the emotional spectrum. Suzanne is again an outcast and is no longer viewed by the others in a favorable light. The favorite of one mother superior becomes the scapegoat of the next, and because the sisters are all subject to the authority of the mother superior, they all must follow suit. This episode in which Suzanne is ostracized is marked morbid scenes of sado-masochism, as reported by the heroine:

> Il faut entendre la langue des couvents pour connaître l'espèce de menace contenue dans ces derniers mots. Deux religieuses relevèrent le suaire [éteignirent les cierges] et me laissèrent trempée jusqu'à la peau de l'eau dont elles m'avaient malicieusement arrosée. Mes habits se séchèrent sur moi, je n'avais pas de quoi me rechanger.[187]

From this point on Suzanne begins to rebel. These lines sound a new theme; Suzanne's recognition of injustice and that of dramatic *anagnorisis*.

> Une autre ajouta qu'à certaines prières je grinçais les dents et que je frémissais dans l'église ; qu'à l'élévation du St. Sacrement je me tordais les bras ; une autre, que je foulais le Christ aux pieds et que je ne portais plus mon rosaire (qu'on m'avait volé ; que je proférais des blasphèmes je n'ose vous répéter ; toutes, qu'il se passait en moi quelque chose qui n'était pas naturel, et qu'il fallait en donner avis au grand vicaire ; ce qui fut fait.[188]

Suzanne refuses to flog herself and by this defiant act she dramatically opposes the new authority. She insists that instead that she will follow the authority of the constitution of the convent: "Je lus les Constitutions, je les relus, je les savais par coeur".[189] Prompted by the fear of persecution, she is quick to try to establish

---

biblical namesake, Suzanne Simonin experiences injustices including sexual harassment. Diderot's knowledge of this story is clearly shown by his discussion of the painting *Suzanne suprise par deux Vieillards* by Jean-Louis-François Lagrenée exhibited in the Salon of 1763, and in his Salon of 1765 discussion of the painting of Suzanne by Carle van Loo. The parallels to Diderot's Suzanne are patently clear.

[187] Diderot, *La Religieuse*, 159.

[188] Diderot, *La Religieuse*, 165–6.

[189] Diderot, *La Religieuse*, 129.

her knowledge of authority. Suzanne has learned an important lesson from her own family, especially from the example of law and authority. The theme of psychological *anagnorisis* is carried through when Suzanne states that she is going to follow the law: "Voilà les engagements que j'ai pris, et je n'en ai point pris d'autres".[190] She recognizes the power of the law and makes the decision to contest the ways of the church and her treatment in the convent by going through the channel of the law. Her resolve is also reinforced by her intention to exercise her own power of reason "Je vais mettre la raison de mon côté".[191]

It is essential at this point that we consider Suzanne's effort to communicate with the outside world. Suzanne writes a letter to a friend asking for help in contacting a lawyer, an act that makes her even more exceptional in this role of the marginalized women. Suzanne manages to maintain a relationship with one sister, to whom she conveys a piece of paper relating all her sorrows. Sister Sainte-Ursule, a nun from a family of means, has connections in the world outside the convent. She puts Suzanne in touch with M. Manouri, a lawyer, and with this act the story begins to take on a different tone. Instead of the pervasive desperation of the second episode, there is now a sense of hopefulness. Describing the injustices perpetrated against her gives Suzanne the impetus to continue, and the kindness shown her by one good soul helps ultimately to sustain her sense of justice: "Je profitai de l'avis de mon amie pour invoquer le secours de Dieu, rassurer mon âme et préparer ma défense".[192] Suzanne comes to believe the legal process to be the most effective way to fight her battle. This is not to say that in her anger she does not consider more extreme methods, such as burning down the convent:

---

[190]Diderot, *La Religieuse*, 130.

[191] Diderot, *La Religieuse*, 130.

[192] Diderot, *La Religieuse*, 167.

> Une question Monsieur, que j'aurais à vous faire, c'est pourquoi à travers toutes les idées funestes qui passent par la tête d'une religieuse désespérée celle de mettre le feu à la maison ne lui vient point.[193]

But in the end reason prevails, and Suzanne pursues her legal defense.

At the conclusion of this episode, Diderot has subjected his character to several different types of alienation. She is physically alienated by the new superior and her cronies, then by her friends, until she has but one friend left who contacts her only in secret. Suzanne is persecuted physically and emotionally as the nuns abuse her and take away her worldly possessions. She is pushed to extremes by Sœur Sainte-Christine, and, though she never totally succumbs, she finally begins to exhibit traits of someone who has been continually persecuted:

> J'étais couchée à terre, la tête et le dos appuyés contre un des murs, les bras croisés sur la poitrine, et le reste de mon corps étendu fermait le passage, lorsque l'office finit, et que les religieuses se présentèrent pour sortir. La première s'arrêta tout court ; les autres arrivèrent à sa suite ; la supérieure se douta de ce que c'était, et dit : "Marchez sur elle ce n'est qu'un cadavre".[194]

It is in this passage where Suzanne finally confronts the possibility of a veritable mental breakdown. Suzanne has been able to use the powerful defense of denial up until this point in the novel. Yet it is in these moments, paradoxically, that Suzanne acts with the greatest clarity. She becomes angry, and her anger gives her self-definition. Her self-knowledge supports her sense of reason and gives her the strength to persevere. We see a shift in Suzanne's resolve; she has chosen to survive as an act of defiance. She also begins to exhibit the first stages of an instinctual survival tactic. This approach is a phenomenon often seen in victims of persecution: temporary acceptance of punishment without opposition: "J'évitai des peines et je supportai plus patiemment celles qui me venaient".[195]

---

[193] Diderot, *La Religieuse*, 134.

[194] Diderot, *La Religieuse*, 162.

[195] This psychological defense mechanism which is commonly referred to as "identification with the aggressor" is also common among battered victims and hostages. This term

Coupled with the blatant anti-church message, the choice of a nun as protagonist is indeed intriguing. Once separated from society, a nun is supposed to accommodate to convent life. She is imagined to live without controversy or conflict, for she takes a vow of strict obedience. Generally, individuality is discouraged in the cloister, but Suzanne's behavior is contrary to all expectations.[196] Her choice to take decisive action presents an early sign that Suzanne will not assume an apathetic stance and this in turn produces an unusual sense of optimism for the reader. Struggle is linked with the powers of the super-ego and Suzanne offers a strong example of this reliance on the super-ego in her contemplation of suicide. This theme is also pervasive in the end of the book where the imagery of death takes over with an emphasis on the color white[197]:

> J'entre au service d'une blanchisseuse chez laquelle je suis actuellement. Je reçois le linge et le repasse... La douleur de ma chute se fait sentir. Mes jambes sont enflées et je ne saurais faire un pas, je travaille assise, car j'aurais à peine me tenir debout...[198]

Remarkably, the threat of death and the theme of continual degradation, as stated earlier, do not color the book with a nihilistic or even pessimistic viewpoint. After portraying the most desperate of situations, Diderot shows Suzanne as psychologically capable of coming back to a lucid state of reason. Even facing death, she is exemplary because she attains her goal of leaving the convent. Paradoxically her qualities of strength and conviction contribute to Suzanne's marginalization. Such strength in the face of persecution is exceptional, and

---

is used by psychologists and psychotherapists when referring to patients that exhibit extreme apathy. Flat affect is a symptom of many mental illnesses including Battered Women's Syndrome. For further definition see: Maria Roy, *Battered Women: A Psychosociological Study of Domestic Violence* (New York: Van Nostrand Reinhold, 1977).

[196] The importance of the convent as a place for marginal to form their own marginal group is discussed at length in: Foucault, *Histoire de la Folie à l'âge classique*, 124–49.

[198] Diderot, *La Religieuse*, 284.

Diderot's perspective convinces us that exceptional people are often singled out for persecution and marginalization. Diderot provides two responses to the question of why this story seems larger than life. First, the fierce struggle for survival against all odds, recounted by the heroine in her letters, adds a surrealistic dimension to the story. Diderot achieves this effect by heightening all of our senses with his use of language and depictions of exaggerated situations. Second, the elements of melodrama, evoked by vivid clinical descriptions and by expressions of Suzanne's will to survive, add to the story's romantic and fictional qualities. All of these acts prove to be types of *forced* marginalization.

In the third episode, the themes of victimization and persecution add additional emotional dimensions to Diderot's depiction of *marginality*. It is ironic that what keeps Suzanne *marginal* is her opposition to being marginalized from all of her contexts. She is troubled by being excluded from her family of origin, and remarkably she never wavers from the belief that she is not suited for convent life. Suzanne tolerates life in the cloister in the first episode because it is made tolerable by the Mère de Moni. She rejects her vows in the second episode because of the mental and physical threats she has already experienced in the cloistered life. The third episode reveals Suzanne in a state of psychological denial; throughout this Suzanne remains unbroken and even after the failure of her court case she goes on with her life. Suzanne is then forced to contend with the sexual advances of her new mother superior. It is in reaction to these advances that she makes that fateful decision to escape no matter the cost. Suzanne's fate is a lonely death in a laundry, but she has won a victory of sorts, for she is free.

Because she dies after her flight to freedom, Suzanne becomes a tragic heroine. At the same time, she embodies one of the primary representations of the *marginal* individual in eighteenth-century society. She is also exceptional in that she makes use of uses her powers of reason and persuasion to attempt to escape her seeming destiny. Therefore, applying a definition of physical alienation for Suzanne's case, though accurate, would be incomplete. The category of physical alienation does not take into account many important aspects of Suzanne's persecution and of her reaction to it. Her process of self-actualization, her attempt at empowerment, and her use of reason all contribute to the process of *forced* marginalization. *La Religieuse* brings the reader into the dimension of the alter-self and in so doing one is put in a position of emotional empowerment. Suzanne is a most unusual heroine, especially for her time. She is at once a martyr in the Christian tradition, a scapegoat in the biblical sense and a sacrifice like Iphegenia in the Ancient Greek tradition who is sent to death by her father Agamemnon. Suzanne's experience of forced alienation, and her psychological and physical reactions to it all fit into the larger category of marginalization, and what is most significant in the depiction of Suzanne's *marginality* is her struggle against it.

In conclusion, Suzanne's story of persecution plays a key role in Diderot's attempt to identify and define the range of concepts represented by our modern notion of *marginality*. His depiction of the character of Suzanne Simonin, in particular, sheds light on the process of the *forced* marginalization of a woman defined by society as illegitimate. *La Religieuse* is, therefore, pivotal in Diderot's artistic and scientific exploration of the issue of marginalization and its consequences.

Chapter Four
Diderot's Unholy Grail:
The Bizarre and Unraveled Quest

This chapter is an investigation of Diderot's interpretation of biological predeterminisim and its roots in French Enlightenment philosophy. Diderot's quest can be considered an "unholy" one, for as he promoted scientific examination of all that was marginal, he simultaneously deemphasized the role of religion as a predetermining force. For this study I present diverse examples within a wide array of Diderot's philosophical and scientific works, including *Les Eléments de physiologie, Pensées sur l'interprétation de la nature, La Lettre sur les Aveugles, La Lettre sur les sourds et les muets, Pensées sur l'interprétation de la nature, Le Rêve de d'Alembert,* and the *Encyclopédie.*[199] All of these works provide us with a diverse sampling of philosophical thought which demonstrates a strong emphasis on the experimental process. These works span a period of over three decades as Diderot explored the notion of the dispossessed on many different levels and in many different forms while formulating and defining concepts known today as alienation, socio-economic alienation, and the theory of *the other* in works dating from (*Lettre sur les aveugles,* 1749)) until his very late works, psychologically (*Les Eléments de physiologie,* 1782). In this chapter, as I focus on theory and methodology as well as on Diderot's use of special terminology, I follow a thematic approach particularly in regard to Diderot's use of the terms *bizarre* and *décousu.* Further aspects of Diderot's attempt to shape a definition of *marginality* emerge clearly from the following analysis of his more speculative works.

---

[199] Denis Diderot, *Encyclopédie,* First Edition, Facsimile, ed. Jean Varloot, Oeuvres Complètes (Cambridge MA: Houghton Library Rare Book Collection, 1812). For this specific part of the study, I used a facsimile of the first edition in attempt to examine the most authentic definition available.

Epistemology

Bizarre, décousu and Related Terms

The eighteenth-century task of defining concepts often took the form of the search for roots and origins in language. Thus we find the roots of Diderot's epistemology in his articles of the *Encyclopédie*. Diderot questions the basis of knowledge itself and formulated the very concept upon which we now judge genius, eccentricity, and often madness, as evidenced by the article entitled *génie* in the *Encyclopédie*.[200] Nonconformity is treated repeatedly, within the rubrics of such terms as *original, monstre, génie*, and *bizarre*. In fact, as stated in the introduction, Diderot used the French words *génie, monstre, bizarre* and *original* in a way that is similar to today's sense of *marginal* in both French and English.[201]

From early in his career as a *philosophe, bizarre* and *décousu* are key terms used in Diderot's search for truth. This quest is the framework for understanding the use of these complex and rich words. According to Diderot, that which appears as truth is not necessarily perfect. Truth can be found in an imperfect state and according to Diderot, it is often found in the state of being "unraveled" or *décousu*. *Décousu* in French literally means "unraveled", but it is also a type of unhinging, a disjointed purposeful unraveling used to reveal truth. Though not episodic as in some of the forms of *décousu*, unraveling is habitual and biological in the genius. What more natural way to observe harmony with the world than from the what Diderot describes in his *Le Rêve de d'Alembert* as the *délire philosophique?*

The French word *bizarre* is used repeatedly by Diderot in philosophy, science, and literature, and the word *bizarre* in the context of the French Enlightenment was used much the same way as the word is today in both French and in English. In the *Encyclopédie* article Diderot uses *"Bizarre, fantasque,*

---

[201] See definition of *"génie"* Denis Diderot, *Encyclopédie* , OC.

[202] The debate on the origins of language as contextualized in the eighteenth century is discussed by Hans Aarslef in his article "The tradition of Condillac: The origin of Language in the Eighteenth Century and the Debate in the Berlin Academy" *From Locke to Saussure: Essays on the Study of Language and Intellectual History.*(Minneapolis: U Minnesota P, 1982) 147-160.

capricieux, quinteux, and *bourru,*" to provide a working definition of this word. He furthers the definition in this way :

> Termes qui marquent tous un défaut dans l'humeur ou l'esprit ; par lequel on s'éloigné de la manière d'agir ou de penser du commun des hommes. *Le fantasque* est dirigé dans sa conduite et dans ses jugements par des idées chimériques qui lui font exiger des choses une sorte de perfection dont elle ne sont pas susceptibles, ou qui lui font remarquer en elles des défauts que personne n'y voit que lui ; *le bizarre,* par une pure affectation de ne rien dire ou faire de singulier ; le capricieux, par un défaut des principes qui l'empêche de se fixer ; *le quinteux,* par des révolutions subites de tempérament qui l'agitent, et *le bourru,* par une certaine rudesse qui vient moins de fond que de d'éducation. *Le fantasque* ne va point sans le chimérique ; *le bizarre* sans l'extraordinaire ; *le capricieux* sans l'arbitraire ; *le quinteux* sans le périodique ; *le bourru,* sans le maussade et tous ces caractères sont incorrigibles.[202]

In the description above, *bizarre* takes on the meaning of "out of the ordinary or peculiar". With these very dense and layered connotations, *bizarre* additionally can mean of unhinged or outside.

The *Pensées sur l'interprétation de la nature* is a philosophical work that deals with science as well as with the method of reasoning. The word *bizarre* occurs several times in the *Pensées sur l'interprétation de la nature,* and always in strategic positions such as in *Pensées* XXIV-XXV and *Pensée* XXX. In the section *Pensée* XXX, we see that Diderot uses this term to convey several themes, all under the umbrella of *marginality.* Looking back to the definition in the *Encyclopédie,* there are at least four terms that Diderot employs interchangeably and are synonymous with *bizarre; fantasque, capricieux, quinteux, bourru.*[203] Wilda Anderson explains Diderot's use of the key term *bizarre* in this way:

> Whether Diderot was describing the behavior of natural philosophers or characterizing his own text, bizarre usually signaled a move or a connection that is not logically supportable at all. The description of the successfully

---

[202] Diderot, *Textes choisis de l'Encyclopédie,* 191.

[203] Diderot, *Textes choisis de l'Encyclopédie,* s.v. "Bizarre".

trained natural philosopher finally provided in *Pensée* XXX shows us that *bizarre* all along has been implicitly used to designate what appears incongruous or arbitrary to the uninitiated eye.[204]

This definition of *bizarre* confirms Diderot's use of the word as close to that of *marginal* and suggests that it is not only Diderot who was unaware of a current to move towards a category of all things *marginal*. Diderot used the term *bizarre* and related terms in this particular context in order to describe natural nonconformity. The end result could be chaotic and bizarre, yet is simply part of a result of experimentation and natural process.

Pensée XXV

Je dis *analogue* ou *bizarre*, parce que tout a son résultat dans la nature ; l'expérience la plus extravagante, ainsi que pour la plus raisonnée. La philosophie expérimentale, qui ne présuppose rien, est toujours contente de ce qui lui vient ; la philosophie rationnelle est toujours instruite, lors même que ce qu'elle s'est proposé ne lui vient pas.[205]

Nature and science have a commonality: both guard the secret of truth. In general terms, the truth is hidden and needs to be unraveled and explored. The notion of *marginality* is intimated in all of Diderot's work, and he addressed the notion of truth in much the same way. Aram Vartanian highlights this point:

A more recent writer on Diderot has approached the post-scriptum from a very different angle, seeing in it a general attitude of skepticism favorable to the search for truth.[206]

Vartanian goes on to explain that the post-scriptum to the *Pensées* is a three tiered text and cannot be simply interpreted, but rather needs to be decoded.

---

[204] Anderson, *Dream*, 22.

[205] Denis Diderot, *Pensées sur l'interprétation de la nature,* ed. Jean Varloot, Œuvres Complètes (Paris: Hermann, 1978), 45.

[206] Aram Vartanian, "The Preamble to Diderot's *Pensées sur l'Interprétation de la Nature*: A Decoding," *Romantic Review*, January 1985, 24. This comment is made in reference to Diderot's *post-scriptum* of the *Pensées*

Examples of a similar quest for truth include the following lines from *Le Rêve de d'Alembert*. Through his character of the doctor Bordeu, Diderot is literally describing what it means to achieve results through this method:

> BORDEU. Qu'est-ce qui circonscrit votre étendue réelle, la vraie sphère de votre sensibilité ?
> MADlle DE L'ESPINASSE. Ma vue et mon toucher.[207]

Here the character of de L'Espinasse underscores the importance of seeing and touching in order to offer scientific proof. Because Diderot was dedicated to revealing the truth, he examined closely the methodology by which one might reach a conclusion. He believed that truth may be found within the process of arriving at a conclusion, as much as in the formal conclusion itself.

Related directly to his idea of the significance of demonstration, Diderot believed that the *how* stage of discovery was most important. Diderot's idea of *marginality* is shown through a display of examples in his more speculative works. Cassirer insists that the importance of the method of discovery becomes most evident when Diderot ponders evolution:

> We cannot know from general concepts how it is possible for one material object to affect another, any more than we can gain a clear insight into the genesis of our ideas. In the one case as in the other we must be satisfied if we can verify the *what* without any knowledge of the *how*. To ask *how* we think and feel how our limbs obey the command of our will, is to inquire into the mystery of creation.[208]

Diderot took the search for truth most seriously, examining the very fundamentals of creation. He often expressed the view that it is in a state of being unraveled and therefore *marginal* that one arrives at the purest truth. In *Le Rêve de d'Alembert* when d'Alembert wakes from his dream he says to Bordeu and Mlle de l'Espinasse : "Qu'est-ce que cette liberté, qu'est-ce que cette volonté de l'homme

---

[207] Diderot, *Œuvres Complètes*, 157.

[208] Cassirer, *Enlightenment*, 54.

qui rêve ?" [209]   Here it becomes evident that Diderot had confidence in the relevance of dreams. There is liberty in the dream state, and this freedom of thought is one pathway to finding the truth. To Diderot the truth is rarely self-evident. In Diderot's fiction most characters are in a state of *"unraveling,"* or delirium, addressing one another and often arguing in a dialectical fashion that could be likened to process.

The dialogue about the discovery of truth in the dream state and its merits are a central theme in *Le Rêve de d'Alembert*, as Bordeu comments: "C'est-à-dire que vous pensez que le mensonge a ses avantages et la vérité ses inconvénients ?"[210] The other side of truth is the lie, which in many contexts has merit, for it is a paradoxical mirror as in the character of Rameau's nephew. This is because lies reflect the truth, for they are its opposites. This idea is represented and underscored in yet another type of process which according to Diderot leads to the discovery of truth:

> Lui. Mais ce n'est pas pour dire la vérité ; au contraire, c'est pour bien dire le mensonge que j'ambitionne votre talent. Si je savais écrire ; fagoter un livre, tourner une épître dédicatoire, bien enivrer un sot de son mérite ; m'insinuer auprès des femmes.[211]

A lie can be equated with what Diderot considered to be *bizarre* in that lies are grotesque misrepresentations of the truth. That which appears to be absolute truth is not, for truth is found in the state of being unraveled in its most crude state of being, or *décousu* ("qui est sans suite, sans liaison," according to *Robert*).[212] Therefore, according to this theory, truth is actually a process rather than an end-product. Diderot locates truth in the method of experimentation as much as in

---

[209] Diderot, *Œuvres Complètes*, 184.

[210] Diderot, *Œuvres Complètes*, 187.

[211] Diderot, *Le Neveu*, 177.

[212] Robert, s.v. "Décousu".

the process of painting. It is revealed in the process of putting things together, or more precisely putting things back together, after their having been taken apart. In *Le Rêve de d'Alembert*, Dr Bordeu reveals the following thoughts about the eternal quality of truth:

> BORDEU. Mais les avantages du mensonge sont d'un moment et ceux de la vérité sont éternels ; mais les suites fâcheuses de la vérité, quand elle en a passent vite, et celles du mensonge ne finissent qu'avec lui.[213]

This is yet another instance when we find one of Diderot's characters reminding the reader that the mirror which is held up to the lie is the truth. Once a lie is represented as such, the truth becomes obvious. Once again, lies are therefore important because, (in a paradoxical way), they represent the truth.

Pensée XXXI repeats an idea that Diderot also presents in *Le Neveu de Rameau*: The creative process starts with an introspective process and is one manner of becoming familiar with one's own internal strife. According to Diderot we understand that finding truth is a self-initiated process, an internal one, and that each individual goes through a different process. In the *Réfutation suivie de l'ouvrage d'Helvétius intitulé l'Homme* Diderot explains his idea of process when seeking truth. The following example accentuates the value of introspection and suggests that truth is found within the individual:

> La fable a caché la vérité au fond d'un puits si profond, qu'il n'est pas donné à tous les yeux de l'y apercevoir. J'appuie le philosophe sur les bords de ce puits ; il regarde : d'abord il n'aperçoit que des ténèbres ; peu à peu ces ténèbres semblent perdre de leur épaisseur ; il croit entrevoir la Vérité : son coeur en tressaille de joie, mais bientôt il reconnaît son erreur, ce qu'il a pris pour la Vérité ne l'était pas. Son âme se flétrit, mais cependant il ne se décourage pas ; il frotte ses yeux, il redouble de contention ; il vient un moment où il s'écrie avec transport : C'est elle...et ce l'est en effet, ou ce ne l'est pas. Il ne la cherche pas à l'aventure ; ce n'est point un aveugle qui tâtonne, c'est un homme clairvoyant qui a longtemps réfléchi sur la meilleure manière d'user de ses yeux selon les différentes circonstances. Il essaye ces méthodes ; et lorsqu'il s'est bien convaincu de leur insuffisance,

---

[213] Diderot, *Œuvres Complètes*, 187.

que fait-il ? Il en cherche d'autres. Alors il ne regarde plus au fond du puits, il regarde en lui-même ; c'est là dont on peut se cacher dans un puits, et les ruses différents dont on peut user pour en faire sortir la Vérité qui s'y est retirée.[214]

Type of introspection mentioned above starts from within but is then communicated externally, as Diderot says in Pensée XXXI: "les développer aux autres." Genius can be discovered in the second step of the process which is communication.

Diderot's reflections in the *Salons* are frequently parenthesized with the same repetition of *bizarre* and *décousu* as in his other works. The author himself refers to one of the chapters of the *Essais* as "*Mes pensées bizarres sur le dessin.*"[215] To Diderot the representation of the grotesque was equally capable of expressing the truth. This raw reality, as presented in paintings like *The Dead Skate* by Chardin, was appreciated by Diderot because of the truthfulness of such paintings. To him, beauty in art was but one expression of truth. For this reason alone it would be interesting and valuable to pursue an investigation of *marginality* in Diderot's descriptions of art. Also in this context Diderot describes his own stream of consciousness, and professes the necessity of unraveling, or letting oneself go to pieces in the creative process. The truth derived from the observation of art is different from scientific truth because it is subjective. There is still an emphasis on process and on explaining the cause and effect of certain situations.[216]

Through all of his writing Diderot also seeks to demonstrate that scientific knowledge is a natural rather than an ordered progression. Similarly in the context of art Diderot says: "Sa palette est l'image du chaos," and this could be interpreted

---

[214] Diderot, *Réfutation*, 617.

[215] Diderot, *Essais sur la peinture*, 343.

[216] This kind of artistic presentation harkens back to the seventeenth-century emphasis on *apparence*. Yet the importance is not in the convention of the art, but in its ability to represent the truth.

as a state of *unraveling.* [217] Diderot saw visual art as one way of expressing truth, especially through the presentation of the *bizarre.* He confirms this point in the *Essais sur la Peinture* : "

> Si les causes et les effets nous étaient évidents, nous n'aurions rien de mieux à faire que de représenter les êtres tels qu'ils sont. Plus l'imitation serait parfaite et analogue aux causes, plus nous en serions satisfaits.[218]

This passage showcases the belief held by Diderot that what was *grotesque* or *bizarre* should not be hidden, but viewed as part of a totality in nature. This holds true for all disciplines into which Diderot delved. In his study and observation of art Diderot speaks of the process of artistic expression in the *Salons* as the *"préparation de l'âme."* He believed this process was introspective, and that the product should please the eye as well as the heart, and that to arrive at the final artistic product the artist must embrace chaos as well as harmony. With this insight, Diderot constitutes a major force in the emergence of a new and critical appreciation for visual art. Herbert Dieckmann helps us put this important step into an historical perspective:

> A work of art is no longer judged by the degree of conformity with traditional patterns and rules, but by the degree of delight it gives, and the delight is caused, not by rational structure and its intellectual simplicity, but by the free play of imagination and emotion. At the same time a keen interest in the creative powers of the artist and in the psychological process of creation awakens.[219]

Diderot's aesthetic challenged the traditional notions of beauty by recommending the depiction of irregular and unpleasant objects due to the reality of their existence in everyday life. Art and sculpture follow protocols distinct from those of science. Questions such as: "Does real evil exist in God's universe?" and

---

[217] Diderot, *Essais sur la peinture*, 344.

[218] Diderot, *Essais sur la peinture*, 344.

[219] Herbert Dieckmann, "Diderot's Conception of Genius," *Journal of the History of Ideas* 2, no. 2 (April 1941): 154.

"Is there a physical manifestation of evil in the natural universe?" preoccupied the Materialists, and the concept of the *bizarre* evolved out of the need to respond to these questions.

The *bizarre* represents a construct of Diderot's philosophy that is parallel in many respects to the modern concept of *marginality*. The word *bizarre* is used in all the different typologies of *marginality* including the types of *self-imposed*, *forced*, and *biologically-predetermined*. Among his many contributions to science, philosophy, and art, Diderot's interest in the origins of genius, and his materialistic philosophy combined in order to produce what amounts to a study of marginalization in mid-eighteenth century France. The end result of Diderot's attempt to understand *marginality* is a rich ensemble of writing that exhibits the unraveling process, and has at its core an avid and dedicated quest for truth.

In the fragment below Diderot explains the process of discovery as "une chaîne d'expériences." Many of the themes that relate to *marginality* come together in Diderot's *Interpretation*. In this next portion of *Pensée* VII, we have a clear illustration of Diderot's theory of methodology and the most complete description of the process of discovery:

Pensée VII

Tant que les choses ne sont que dans notre entendement, ce sont nos opinions ; ce sont des notions qui peuvent être vraies ou fausses, accordées ou contredites. Elles ne prennent de la consistance qu'en se liant aux êtres extérieurs. Cette liaison se fait ou par une chaîne ininterrompue de raisonnements qui tiennent d'un bout à l'observation, et de l'autre à l'expérience ; ou par une chaîne d'expériences dispersées d'espace en espace entre raisonnements, comme des poids sur la longueur d'un fil suspendu par ses deux extrémités. Sans ces poids, le fil deviendrait le jouet de la moindre agitation qui se ferait dans l'air.

This passage from *Le Rêve de d'Alembert* purports that there is harmony in the chaos of the *unraveled*, and underscores the need for both order and disorder. There is a chain (process) set up, and the tension between these two poles is necessary for the dialectical process to function.

MADlle DE L'ESPINASSE. Docteur, approchez-vous. Imaginez une araignée au centre de sa toile. Ébranlez un fil, et vous verrez l'animal alerte accourir. Eh bien, si les fils que l'insecte tire de ses intestins, et y rappelle quand il lui plaît, faisaient partie de lui-même ? ...[220]

La physique expérimentale, Diderot explains, has an order that is necessary and prescribed, whereas *la philosophie naturelle* and *la philosophie expérimentale* exhibit more spontaneous and chaotic forms of reasoning. It is in keeping with his views that both *la philosophie expérimentale* and *la philosophie naturelle* are important methods of discovery, yet Diderot felt the need to parenthesize them with excuses. *Le Rêve de d'Alembert* is but one instance where Diderot constantly refers to the state of being unraveled. He uses dreaming and crazy ideation to demonstrate the notion of *décousu*. Harmony is located in the idea of being in chaos because of two opposite movements, the *(décousu)* unraveling, and the *(enchaînement)* or putting things back together. Diderot's idea of voluntary and involuntary systems conforms to Anderson's idea that phenomena are linked to each other logically and physically. For Diderot these systems are interdependent.

In many instances, references to the "délire philosophique" precede or follow scientific or philosophical digressions. *L'état de l'extase* is similar to *le délire philosophique* as discussed here in *Le Rêve d'Alembert* by Dr. Bordeu:

> BORDEU. Par exemple, si l'origine du faisceau rappelle toutes les forces à lui, si le système entier se meut pour ainsi dire à rebours, comme je crois qu'il arrive dans l'homme qui médite profondément, dans le fanatique qui voit les cieux ouverts, dans le sauvage qui chante au milieu des flammes, dans l'extase, dans l'aliénation volontaire ou involontaire...[221]

All the elements of Diderot's line of questioning come into play in this one compact example. The ideas of origins and of biological predisposition to certain behaviors are expressed in the context of an entire system. Here too, the state of

---

[220] Diderot, *Œuvres Complètes*, 140.

[221] Diderot, *Œuvres Complètes*, 171. Ellipsis original.

unraveling is put in terms of the fanatic who sees the skies open and the wild man who sings while being enveloped by fire. The *marginalization* that takes place for this type of person in the altered state is called alienation here, and it seems inconsequential whether it is self-imposed or not.

Monsters and Demons

Pensée XXX makes it clear that the perception of something *bizarre* is a local reaction. Culture dictates the norm and tolerates what is categorized as *marginal*. When we compare *Pensée* VII to *Pensée* XXX we see that Diderot employed the term *bizarre* to designate that which appears incongruous or arbitrary to the uninitiated eye. "*Marginal*s" are *démons*, yet they are familiar, thus only a little *marginal*. Questioning the human desire for familiarity, is a conflict that permeates the work of Diderot and provides a link to understanding of the range of degrees of *marginality* to *lui* of *Le Neveu de Rameau*. For it is in *Le Neveu de Rameau* we see the first concrete example of the notion that the more familiar, or intimate someone is, the less the emotional distancing.

The desire for familiarity is also an emotion that Diderot refers to in the scientific realm in reference to methodology. In the fragment below Diderot highlights the importance of the experimental process and *tâtonnement* (perception by means of touch.) Once again he references Socrates in connection to methodology:

Pensée XXX
La grande habitude de faire des expériences donne aux manouvriers d'opérations les plus grossiers un pressentiment qui a le caractère de l'inspiration. Il ne tiendrait qu'à eux de s'y tromper comme Socrate, et de l'appeler un démon familier.[222]

The context of this quote can be applied to much of Diderot's work for the method of *expérience* or experimentation initiated by intuition was of great import to him. In the eighteenth-century sorcerers and necromancers, who professed to

---

[222] Diderot, *Pensées*, 47–8.

call up the dead, were said to hear a" familiar spirit."[223] In this instance Diderot again looks to Socrates who was frequently described as a "mystic," and who had an inner "voice," or a familiar *daemon*. According to Plato the daemon gave only negative admonitions, which may account for the theory of some writers that the "voice" was merely that of conscience.

Just as Diderot used the language of spiritual possession to refer to the subjective experience of artistic and intellectual inspiration so too did he draw from the language of folklore and superstition to describe wholly natural phenomenon such as in the use of the term *monstre* as a natural deviation from the norm. Prior to the eighteenth century monsters were understood by many in the Western world to be supernatural manifestations of evil in the universe. At the time Diderot was actively writing, monsters were beginning to be seen as anomalies of nature. When Diderot says "la nature ne fait rien d'incorrect" in the *Essais*, we are given to understand that Diderot does not subscribe to the view that monsters represent the action of malefic forces in the universe.[224] Perfection is found in harmony, and as stated earlier, harmony for Diderot is found especially in the inner tension of chaos. In his view chaos at times produces mutations and as chaos is part of nature, with all of its variations, nature is as it should be. This short description from the *Essais sur la peinture* confirms this idea:

> La nature ne fait rien d'incorrect. Toute forme belle ou laide a sa cause, et de tous les êtres qui existent, il n'y en a pas un qui ne soit comme il doit être.[225]

---

[223] Diderot demonstrates his awareness of the Biblical references to the "familiar spirit" in Deut. 18:1, 2 Kings 21:6, Chronicles 33:6, Lev. 19:1

[224] Diderot, *Essais sur la peinture*, 343.

[225] Denis Diderot, *Essais sur la peinture*, ed. Gita M. May, Œuvres Complètes (Paris: Hermann, 1984), 343.

Instead, Diderot subscribes to the materialist viewpoint that accidents of nature were part of the natural order. Materialism redefined "natural" in such a way that it effectively surrendered the very norms men sought to defend against the threat of monsters.[226]

It was then up to Diderot to begin to redefine what was meant by the natural order. Diderot derived his idea of materialism by denial of the mind-body opposition. Jacques Proust explains this in his work *Diderot et L'Encyclopédie*:

> L'âme de l'homme est indissolublement unie à son corps ; nous avons donc, avec les objets extérieurs, des rapports semblables à ceux que les animaux ont avec les mêmes objets.[227]

The idea that the mind and the body were not separate entities was certainly conjectural then it is as today. Explaining these conjectures was one of Diderot's tasks in the *Interprétation* and is one key element in his effort to redefine the natural order. Later in the *Eléments de Physiologie* he would delve even deeper into speculation, making some key methodological proposals.

In the beginning of *La Suite d'un entretien entre M. d'Alembert et M. Diderot,* Diderot initiates a discussion pondering the nature of matter and the question of what is natural. This transition marks the beginning of a series of dialectical questions that probe the origins of biological diversity.

> J'avoue qu'un être qui existe quelque part et qui ne correspond à aucun point de l'espace ; un être qui est inétendu et qui occupe de l'étendue ;...un être d'une nature aussi contradictoire est difficile à admettre. Mais d'autres obscurités...[228]

This passage occurs at a point where Diderot's consideration of materialism demonstrates an effort to delineate between matter and non-matter and is also

---

[226] Emita Hill, "The Theme of Monsters in the Works of Denis Diderot", (Harvard University Press, 1972), 154.

[227] Jacques Proust, *Diderot et L'Encyclopédie* (Paris: Armand Colin, 1967), 289.

[228] Diderot, *Œuvres Complètes*, 161.

related to his conceptualization of biological predeterminisim. Thus the concept of *genius* takes place within the discussion of biological diversity.

There is yet another connection to the notion of biologically predetermined diversity in Diderot's investigation of the view of monsters in eighteenth century France. A portion of the discussion of nature in the *Entretien* as well as in the following description of *Monstre* from the *Encyclopédie* describe monsters as accidents of nature; thus they are by their own definition natural:

> Il y a bien des sortes de monstres par rapport à leurs structures, et on se sert de deux hypothèses pour expliquer la production des monstres : la première suppose des œufs originairement et éventuellement monstrueux : la seconde cherche les seules causes accidentelles la raison de toutes ces conformations.[229]

Diderot makes a link between monsters of nature and human beings who are "monstrous" in various aspects. While *Le Rêve de d'Alembert* depicts freaks of nature, many more of Diderot's fictional characters present aspects of self-alienation. The self-alienation evident in Diderot's fiction is a direct criticism of the alienating elements in eighteenth-century society.

Let us consider the basic definition of *monstre* attributed to Diderot in the *Encyclopédie*. Here we can see a few examples of the initiatives he took in the direction of linking these two types of monsters; those in nature and those in society:

> Monstre : Animal qui naît avec une formation contraire à l'ordre de la nature, c'est à dire avec une structure de parties très-différentes de celles qui caractérisent l'espèce des animaux dont il sont.[230]

Diderot's fascination with the subject of *marginality* from a medical or scientific viewpoint led him to an interest in human beings who were different

---

[229] Denis Diderot, *Textes choisis de l'Encyclopédie*, ed. Albert Soboul, Œuvres Complètes (Paris: Editions Sociales, 1952), s.v. "Monstre.".

[230] Diderot, *Textes choisis de l'Encyclopédie*, s.v. "Monstre.".

because of severe organic dysfunctions. These anomalies were referred to as *monstres* in the *Encyclopédie*. In the *Pensées sur l'interprétation de la nature* Diderot records fragmentary ideas connecting them in his own interpretation. There are entire sections devoted to *marginality* of one type or another. Also in the *Eléments de physiologie* he uses his materialist philosophy as a backing for his argument.

Materialists applied natural law to explain what previously was understood by religion as an act of God. The idea that congenital anomalies were biologically determined was new and yet to be proved. Experimentation needed to be developed in order to understand more fully phenomena that looked to the untrained eye like the monstrous creations of God. Diderot considers monsters of nature to be a biological phenomenon rather than a function of God or religion. To emphasize his point, Diderot speaks of the Siamese twins as a biological phenomenon in *Le Rêve de d'Alembert*:

> ...Doublez quelques-uns des brins du faisceau, et l'animal aura deux têtes, quatre yeux, quatre oreilles, trois testicules, trois pieds, quatre bras, six doigts à chaque main. Dérangez les brins du faisceau, et les organes seront déplacés : la tête occupera le milieu de la poitrine, les poumons seront à gauche, le cœur à droite. Collez ensemble deux brins, et les organes se confondront ; les bras s'attacheront au corps ; les cuisses, les jambes et les pieds se réuniront, et vous aurez toutes les sortes de monstres imaginables.[231]

Jennifer Vanderheyen offers a very insightful observation on the importance of twinning and the sense of *the other* in her discussion of *Le Rêve de d'Alembert*. The pair of conjoined twins to which Diderot refers were girls born with their backs conversely connected and thus were in opposite mirror position.

> Although twins are in essence two separate personalities or subjects, the lives of these conjoined twins depend on the unity of the blood source that

---

[231] Denis Diderot, *Œuvres Complètes*, ed. H.Dieckmann, *Le Rêve de d'Alembert* Edited by Herbert Dieckmann (Paris: Hermann, 1975) 150.

connects them and alternately keeps them alive. Each is always "haunted" and inhabited by the other.[232]

In this way, the twins are similar to many of Diderot's other marginals in that they reflect what is "other". With these descriptions Diderot approaches a methodological definition of a subcategory of marginalized individuals: that of biologically predetermined *marginality*, individuals who are deformed, misshapen, or physically disabled fit into this category. Diderot's materialism allows him to reach beyond the confines of a religiously oriented answer to the existence of monsters.

The *Lettre sur les Aveugles* evokes a chaotic picture of the universe that vitiates by its pessimistic nature a sense of hope and continuity. The *Lettre sur les Aveugles* challenges one's ideas of uniformity in the universe. Monsters endanger man's faith in the rationality of nature and in the efficacy of his/her own reason. Even at the beginning of the twenty-first century we are at pains to accept the eighteenth-century idea of nature's indifference or to admit the simultaneous existence of naturally occurring regularity and irregularity.[233]

A clear example of biological difference in Diderot's work is located in *Le Rêve de d'Alembert*. In this particular piece Diderot is fascinated by the variations in nature evoked in his discussion between Mlle de L'Espinasse and Dr. Bordeu. Not only does the discussion point to those who are congenitally different from others, they use the metaphor of *monstre* to begin to explain the difference between the sexes:

MADlle DE L'ESPINASSE. Il me vint une idée bien folle.

---

[232] Jennifer Vanderheyden, *The Function of the Dream and the Body in Diderot's Works*, The Age of Revolution and Romanticism Interdisciplinary Studies. Vol 31(New York: Peter Lang, 2004) 65-66.

[233] According to Diderot's materialism, passions are beneficial. Any restraints, like the boundaries of the Church, are unnecessary. Religion is the product of unnatural constraints. Melancholia is the product of unrealized passion. Diderot's discussion on homosexuality in *La Religieuse* is not clear at times. It seems Diderot is less decided on this issue compared to others. He seems confused between repressed heterosexual desire and repressed sexual passion.

BORDEU. Quelle ?
MADlle DE L'ESPINASSE. L'homme n'est peut-être que le monstre de la femme, ou la femme le monstre de l'homme.[234]

In *Le Rêve de d'Alembert* Diderot moves to a discussion of normative behavior. The idea of a norm is especially pertinent when used in relationship to the concept of genetically predetermined differences in behavior and appearances. As long as materialism could rationalize the existence of monsters, they could be explained as natural. In *Le Rêve de d'Alembert* the question of heredity is revisited in a dialogue about the origins of congenital deformities.

MADlle DE L'ESPINASSE. A-t-on des exemples remarquables de ces difformités originelles autres que les bossus et les boiteux dont on pourrait attribuer l'état maléficié à quelque vice héréditaire ?[235]

At this juncture in *Le Rêve de d'Alembert,* evil in nature was unjustified because it could not be scientifically explained. Once defined, the norm is created, and what is out of the ordinary becomes marginalized. The norm therefore is pre-ordained by biological factors.[236]

Anomalies of nature had a purpose according to Diderot, and not unlike the Rameau's nephew, may indeed be *un peu en marge.* They do however serve a purpose for society. These anomalies, like the nephew, mirror what normalcy is for those who exist within the norm and they tend to make people thankful for what they are not. With these cynical references Diderot seems to be preaching his own kind of tolerance. Emita Hill states how in Diderot's system nature might be aligned with God's laws:

The influence of a Newtonian interpretation of the natural universe necessarily altered men's reactions to the occurrence of physical

---

[234] Diderot, *Oeuvres Complètes*, 152.

[235] Diderot, *Oeuvres Complètes*, 151.

[236] In order to judge what is extraordinary one must have a norm. It is important to note here that what was marginal was used to mirror the norm itself.

monstrosities. An autonomous nature might err in carrying out God's intentions for his universe; he might produce freaks accidentally. A nature ruled by God-given laws might produce only what was reasonable and predictable under those laws.[237]

In the segment above Hill explains that the monster also serves as a base and a vehicle for Diderot's discovery and expression of his new ideas of materialism. Materialism too was at the base of Diderot's general philosophy and was the force that pushed him furthest from the Church. Hill also clarifies how a consideration of monsters and materialism helped form the norm in the middle of the eighteenth century:

> Materialism equates the monster and normal men; it denies any significance to the individual, to his opinions, and even to his existence. But Diderot's characters express their individuality; they imply, through their doubts and affirmations, the belief in norms.[238]

The norm is seen through that which is different. The position that many of Diderot's characters take is outside of the norm in order to prove that such a margin exists. Their behavior or form is often exaggerated and the term *bizarre* is employed in order to heighten the distance between the norm and the marginalized.[239]

Language and the Scientific Method

Why is it that in Diderot's philosophical works we find the most focused descriptions of what he regarded as *marginal*? Perhaps it is because he used these descriptions not merely as an artistic medium, but as a virtual scientific laboratory in his attempt to understand quirky and sometimes troubling behaviors he observed in others and to explore the range of extremes in these behaviors from the peculiar to the deviant. This search is reflective of Diderot's deep interest in science, rooted

---

[237] Hill, "Monsters," 156.

[238] Hill, "Monsters," 50.

[239] Hill, "Monsters," 156.

in his philosophical stance as a materialist. Ernst Cassirer identifies Diderot's materialism with the intensity of interest which the mysteries of biology and heredity held for many of the French Enlightenment philosophers. Here Cassirer emphasizes Diderot's confidence in the power of science:

> In his essay *On the Interpretation of Nature* (1754) Diderot, who was among the thinkers of the eighteenth century probably possessed the keenest sense for all intellectual movements and transitions of that epoch, remarks that the century seems to have reached a decisive turning-point. A great revolution in the field of science is now in the offing.[240]

In *The Philosophy of the Enlightenment* Cassirer further explains that freeing natural science from theological and metaphysical content for some of the *philosophes* appeared to be a simple process.

> The task of freeing natural science from the domination of theology appeared as a relatively simple matter to Enlightenment thought. To accomplish this task it was merely necessary to utilize the heritage of preceding centuries; the separation had already taken place in fact, had now to be realized conceptually.[241]

Yet despite their best efforts, many philosophers of the Enlightenment had a difficult time in separating the spiritual from the scientific. The distinctions between these worlds tended to blur. Suzanne Pucci in *Diderot and a Poetics of Science* points out that the eighteenth century ushered in a shift in thinking that led to a new philosophical agenda:

> A growing emphasis on the natural sciences in the eighteenth century appears to coincide with a particular interest in epistemological distinctions between sense perception and abstract thought. An emphasis, however, on the material world as perceived through the senses and as distinct from abstract thought, presented new problems. How to assure adequation of sense perception with the physical object world without implying

---

[240] Ernst Cassirer, *The Philosophy of the Enlightenment*, (Princeton: Princeton University Press, 1960), 73–4.

[241] Cassirer, *Enlightenment*, 58.

individual distortion and consequently, without blurring the distinctions between the properties of perception and those of the abstract, even arbitrary operations of the mind?[242]

Diderot promoted and embraced this new philosophical stance. Especially with his work on the *Encyclopédie* he became known as a strong proponent of the conceptual changes taking place in the eighteenth century. In all his works Diderot tried to demonstrate the separation between the theological, scientific, and metaphysical worlds.

Diderot himself is given to an introspective process in all of his writings. Yet, perhaps deliberately, he does not explain his method of writing. Rather, the process demonstrates Diderot's confidence in experimental thinking. Cassirer affirms that Diderot was not alone in adopting this method of expression, but participated in a trend of philosophical thought and expression which became increasingly popular at the end of the seventeenth century:

> The modern concept of nature, as its shape becomes increasingly articulate from the Renaissance on and as it seeks philosophical foundation and justification in the great systems of the seventeenth century in-Descartes, Spinoza, and Leibniz-is characterized above all by the new relationships which develop between sensibility and intellect, between experience and thought, between the sensible world and the intelligible world.[243]

Diderot's materialistic philosophy was founded upon a tolerance for disorder in the universe as well as in his own work. The ordered universe was a central claim of religion and something against which Diderot reacted strongly. His reaction rested on a new scientific concept which included the existence of a fundamental force of disorder in the universe and a methodology of its own. Diderot's philosophical work is an investigation that says things by doing them. He rejected the old system in the philosophical medium of expression.

---

[242] Suzanne Pucci, *Diderot and a Poetics of Science,* (New York: Peter Lang, 1986), 73.

[243] Cassirer, *Enlightenment,* 38.

Examples of Diderot's rejection of the old idea of order appear in his descriptions of experimentation such as this one in *Le Rêve de d'Alembert*: [244]

MADlle DE L'ESPINASSE. Un moment, Docteur ; récapitulons. D'après vos principes, il me semble par une suite d'opérations purement mécaniques je réduirais le premier génie de la terre à une masse de chair inorganisée, à laquelle on ne laisserait que la sensibilité du moment, et que l'on ramènerait cette masse informe de l'état de la stupidité le plus profond que l'on puisse imaginer à la condition de l'homme de génie. [245]

Also located in the passage above from *Le Rêve,* Mlle De l'Espinasse continues the discussion of one of Diderot's main obsessions: the theory of genius and its origins. Even in this philosophical discussion about the origins of genius, Diderot presents different sides of the issue. In this context the problematic is whether or not to reduce the idea of the origins of genius to a biologically predetermined factor. At the same time Diderot addresses the idea of a thought process: "une suite d'opérations purement mécaniques". Even in the most purely speculative arenas he still addresses the necessity of proceeding through certain steps to arrive at a conclusion, orderly or not.

Diderot's commentary on biological determinism, on the other hand, is related to his scientific and philosophical queries. Both Diderot's criticism of the age in which he lived and his scientific queries formed part of the central problematic for his materialistic philosophy, leaving the following questions unanswered:

1) Is *marginal* behavior a matter of simple environmental influence or is it an innate proclivity that is decisive in these processes?

---

[244] Diderot tries to contain philosophic and scientific speculation within a materialistic framework. All creatures, according to the materialistic viewpoint, are good. All imperfections, therefore, must result from accidents subsequent to their formation.

[245] Diderot, *Oeuvres Complètes*, 188.

2) Does the environment influence individuals born with certain behaviors to the extent that the behavior becomes internalized and therefore part of the human psychological dynamic?

Marginality played a key role in Diderot's attempt to process ideas pertaining to materialism, and he continually explored different aspects of this notion. At the end of his lifetime, while confined to his bed, Diderot reviewed his treatise on what he saw as a necessary explanation of biological functions in humans. In the *Eléments de Physiologie* Diderot's interest in the biological and organic aspects of *marginality* had grown to great proportions. This treatise is an example of Diderot's speculative writing where questions on *marginality* are represented in a different form from his fictional works. The questions appear, but they are not portrayed by Diderot's usual cast of colorful characters. Instead they are presented in a straightforward and clinical way and expose the more scientific side of the philosopher.

In addition to his work as *philosophe* and *encyclopédiste*, we may now appreciate another dimension of Diderot's accomplishments and insights. In the examples below we see that, while pondering concepts such as alienation and otherness Diderot makes an attempt to define the concept of *marginality* in the discipline of science. It is the striking correlation between Diderot's dialectical arguments and his literary depictions that offers the most convincing proof of this hypothesis. Records of Diderot's ever-evolving philosophical stance, accompanied by important biographical information, add strength to this postulation. Thus we see that Diderot's acute observations of people and society impelled him to attempt to conceptualize and dramatize key processes related to what would be referred to today as *marginality*.

Entendement

In the *Pensées sur l'interprétation de la nature* Diderot gives ample testimony to his shift toward a materialistic way of thinking. Diderot further expounds upon a key notion that distinguished the materialists from other thinkers of the time which is illustrated by their application of the notion of *entendement*.

Pensée XVIII

La véritable manière de philosopher, c'eût été et ce serait d'appliquer l'entendement à l'entendement ; l'entendement et l'expérience aux sens ; les sens à la nature ; la nature à l'investigation des instruments ; les instruments à la recherche et à la perfection des arts qu'on jetterait au peuple pour lui apprendre à respecter la philosophie.[246]

In deepening this analysis, let us consider how the word *entendement* as it is used repeatedly in the *Interprétation,* becomes synonymous with the concept of an introspective process. This is evidenced by the definition in the *Dictionnaire de Trévoux* which reflects its usage in eighteenth-century France.

Entendement : C'est la partie dominante de l'âme, où réside le jugement et l'intelligence. On distingue deux facultés dans l'âme : en tant qu'elle juge, et consent, ainsi la conviction de l'entendement dirige et détermine la volonté.[247]

In the intellectual discourse of eighteenth-century France, the notion of *entendement* was associated with the comprehension of scientific discovery and philosophical reasoning and related to a thought process by which one arrives at a conclusion. In the *Interprétation*, the artistic enterprise of self-expression is problematic for Diderot, but at the core there is a similar emphasis on *process* as there is on science, although the emphasis is somewhat differently shaded in each case.

Diderot's speculative work follows a sophisticated discourse based on open ended experimental process and as such is original and revolutionary. Later philosophical movements such as Existentialism follow a similar trajectory. For

---

[246] Diderot, *Pensées*, 41.

[247] *Dictionnaire de Trévoux*, s.v. "Entendement". The eighteenth-century ideas of rational and reason are approached in this definition through the separation of *âme* and *intelligence*.

example, the word *enchaînement* is used to indicate that there is an actual process within the rantings of Rameau's nephew. It is not so much what the nephew says, but how he says it. He is the *porte-parole* of the bourgeoisie and of many others, expressing what correct society cannot otherwise articulate.

Pensée XXXI

Comment cet esprit se communique-t-il ? Il faudrait que celui qui en est possédé, descendît en lui-même pour reconnaître distinctement ce que c'est, substituer au démon familier des notions intelligibles et claires, et les développer aux autres.[248]

When describing and defining the concept of *process* as Diderot interprets it, one has only to look to *Pensée* XXXI of the *Interprétation* to begin to comprehend what a rich and vast concept it is and how central it is to the core of Diderot's materialistic philosophy. Diderot demonstrates *process* in these works by taking the readers through a series of steps of reasoning. *Enchaînement* has two possible meanings in the works of Diderot. Phenomena are linked to each other physically to form the world, and phenomena are linked to each other logically. The logic is merely the statement or recognition of physical links. Neither type can exist without the other.[249] In the reasoning of the *Interprétation* and the delirium of d'Alembert in *Le Rêve de d'Alembert*, we see the resonance of a creative artistic process, particularly when Diderot discusses *La méthode de la physique expérimentale* in *Pensée* XXIV. He repeatedly refers to method when he states : "L'emploi s'étend à la comparaison, à l'application et à la *combinaison.*"

One section of *Pensée* XXXI, when taken apart, reveals Diderot's notion that experimentation is part of the discovery process. As he presents the idea of experimentation he calls it "Un enchaînement de conjectures." This process of "*enchaînement*" is linked to the original idea in this chapter of the quest for truth.

---

[248] Diderot, *Pensées*, 48.

[249] This idea is referred to in: Wilda Anderson, *Diderot's Dream* (Baltimore: Johns Hopkins University Press, 1990), 40.

Pensée XXXI

S'il trouvait, par exemple, que c'est une facilité de supposer ou d'apercevoir des oppositions ou des analogies, qui a sa source dans une connaissance pratique des qualités physiques des êtres considérées solitairement, ou de leurs effets réciproques, quand on les considère en combinaison ; il éteindrait cette idée ; il l'appuierait d'une infinité de faits qui se présenteraient à sa mémoire ; ce serait une histoire fidèle de toutes les extravagances apparentes qui lui ont passé par la tête.[250]

The illustrative idea of the fragment above from *Pensée* XXXI is that discovery is interchangeable with *process* and that any type of discovery, be it psychological or scientific, goes through a series of steps. The next section of the *Pensée* also points out the importance of every element of discovery. The conclusion is particularly important because of the consequences the observations might hold for other discoveries or experiments.

C'est un tout si précaire et dans les suppositions et dans les conséquences, qu'on a souvent dédaigné de faire ou les observations ou les expériences qu'on en concluait.[251]

This fragment of *Pensée* XXXI reiterates the idea that even in experimentation Diderot was a naturalist, for he found a natural logic inherent in the series of conjectures necessary for experimentation.

Diderot does not go into depth in explaining scientific methodology in the *Lettre sur les Aveugles* as he would later do in his other speculative pieces. In the *Interpretation*, truth derived from science is founded upon the order of proof: one could not overlook the function of arrangement, for doing so would make the very principle of experimentation useless. The *Interpretation* clarifies the points of discovery in the process of experimentation while the *Lettre sur les Aveugles* touches upon the ideas of scientific order and proof. Yet order and truth are addressed in a new way in the *Lettre*. Lester Crocker speaks of the *Lettre* this way:

---

[250] Diderot, *Pensées*, 48–9.

[251] Diderot, *Pensées*, 49.

The letter brings a strong thrust on the part of all men, subjected to communal living and determined by their organic constitution, to impose order in their relationships. The validity of the order so established is not questioned.[252]

In fact, the *Interpretation* unites many diverse facets of Diderot's philosophy. It is in this work that we see the relationship of *genius, bizarre,* and *décousu.* As we have seen, the notion of *genius* greatly preoccupied Diderot and the concepts of order and disorder are fundamental to Diderot's investigation of the origins of genius. According to his understanding of *genius*, the concept of the *bizarre* is at the base of what makes genius effective. To Diderot both notions, *bizarre* and *décousu,* are needed in order to balance out discovery; one is *process* and one is *presentation.* Yet genius is one context wherein Diderot uses the vocabulary of chaos and bizarreness, where any kind of process is confusing and a justification of biological predeterminisim is essential. In the unraveled state, one might be *bizarre*, one might even see *bizarre* things, or make *bizarre* discoveries.

When speaking of process and presentation in Diderot one must remember that they often appear conflated. Christie McDonald in *The Writing of Dialogue* puts forth this explanation when considering a discussion of the eighteenth-century origins of the concept of *genius*:

> One can distinguish here at least two levels at which the problem of artistic interpretation and creation is posed. The first is that of written notation. In this scene, the nephew seems to interpret the score of another composer. The question implicit here, and explicit elsewhere in discussions about the problem of genius, is how the work (the musical score) comes to be and who produces it.[253]

In this illustration, the discussions of process and genius are linked; it is clear that the question of how genius is expressed will be an open ended query. The

---

[252] Crocker, *Chaotic*, 8.

[253] Christie McDonald, *TheDialogue of Writing* (Waterloo, Ontario: Wilfred Laurier University Press, 1984), 93.

next problematic revealed in this analysis will then be *who* merits the title of genius. The *who* is an important part of Diderot's question about the biological inheritance of genius. A genius might be a psychologically disorganized person existing in a state of unraveling, but the genius does not go through the same sort of process as discussed earlier. The type of biologically predetermined marginalized person would therefore exist in a state of unraveling and the life of that person could be likened to a chaotic state of discovery.

Diderot continually emphasizes the importance of investigating the extraordinary, particularly when produced by nature, and this notion carried over into depictions of nature in art. In his view they should not necessarily be realistic, but should evoke the idea of the sublime. Diderot felt justified in conveying this message in his work. Later in his work, he explained the notion of the sublime in relation to the grotesque. He introduced this discussion in very extreme terms therefore linking it to pre-romantic notions. For Diderot, Art is yet another form of paradoxical expression. Diderot's notion of the *bizarre* connotes the idea of "out of the ordinary" and the French term *grotesque* is often used by Diderot as a synonym for *bizarre*, especially in his art criticism. One could say with some degree of certainty that this aspect of the *bizarre* is linked to the pre-romantic notion of the grotesque and the sublime, as Gita May has highlighted in her article "Diderot and Burke: A Study in Aesthetic Affinity." She explains that Diderot understood that the thought-process is affected by the powerful emotions evoked by the sublime, especially those produced by nature:

> Like Burke, Diderot is attracted to awe-inspiring scenes whose qualities evoke lofty thoughts and powerful sentiments, and he too holds that sublimity is a subjective emotion, an inner state of mind, induced by the grand and wild aspects of nature, especially those that reveal mysterious, untamed forces that surround us.[254]

---

[254] Gita May, "Diderot and Burke: A Study in Aesthetic Affinity," Diderot and Burke, *PMLA*, December 1960, 532.

The link between the emotions and the aesthetic impulse was obvious for Diderot. Using the power of the visual to evoke an emotional response is one way to bring about the introspection needed to begin the process that lies at the base of Diderot's dialectic of change. In this way the visual plan functions much like the speculative platform of process in science.

A similar procedure is used in the examination of the *bizarre* and of *monstres*, and this protocol is also used to explain the notion of genius. In other words the extraordinary is set apart from the norm by categorization and definition. It is significant that when Diderot first categorizes the normal thought process, he puts it into perspective by juxtaposing it to that which is considered extraordinary. Another segment of *Pensée* XXXI presents this juxtaposition:

Pensée XXXI
Je dis *extravagances* : car quel autre nom à donner à cet enchaînement de conjectures fondées sur les oppositions ou des ressemblances si éloignées, si imperceptibles, que les rêves d'un malade ne paraissent ni plus *bizarres* ni plus *décousus*. Il n'y a quelque fois pas une proposition qui ne puisse être contredite, soit en elle même, soit dans sa liaison avec celle qui la précède ou qui la suit.[255]

The last part of *Pensée* XXXI is most explicit in its use of *bizarre* and *décousu :* "que les rêves d'un malade ne paraissent ni plus *bizarres* ni plus *décousus.* " This line is clearly a foreshadowing of themes in *Le Rêve de d'Alembert*, where Bordeu expounds on scientific phenomena.[256] The concept of the *bizarre* is elucidated plainly and repeatedly in the passages that play off of the *"délire philosophique."* Mlle de l'Espinasse finally launches the discussion when she comments candidly: "Voilà une espèce assez bizarre."[257] The discussions of the Cyclops and the Siamese twins parenthesize Mlle de l'Espinasse's commentary.

---

[255] Diderot, *Pensées*, 49.

[256] Diderot, *Pensées*, 161–70.

[257] Diderot, *Pensées*, 161.

The word *bizarre*, though basically used in the sense "out of the ordinary," has a particular nuance in each separate context. We have seen in the preceding sections that the word has taken on the meaning of *original*. [258] It seems that this position is not only self-appointed but is also pre-ordained by biology. Yet, as is often the case, Diderot contradicts himself as we have seen in *Le Neveu de Rameau* when the nephew confesses to be just mediocre. Rameau's nephew did not inherit the genius of his uncle, rather he was given to mediocrity: "J'ai donc été; je suis donc fâché d'être mediocre."[259]

Tâtonnement

Diderot seems to inhabit two worlds, that of the natural philosopher and that of the experimental philosopher. The experimental philosopher pays attention to method, process, and culture but the natural philosopher is more spontaneous and knows the world by actively becoming part of it. Diderot's philosophy of materialism is based on the doctrine that all things are reduced to the unity of matter and that every particle is capable of animation and actions. Nature does not necessarily oppose culture, and cannot be assumed at times to be its opposite. In this way Diderot can be considered a natural philosopher as distinct from an experimental philosopher.

Diderot's method as a philosopher exhibits a broad spectrum of opinions. He is very much a part of society and takes part in the culture. At other times he positions himself at a distance and criticizes the norms. He demonstrates the ability to comprehend and to evaluate sympathetically, sometimes accepting new interpretations from others. In his various methods of discovery from dream state

---

[258] Parts of *La Religieuse* and *Le Rêve de d'Alembert* incorporate yet another meaning, closer to that of *original*. Diderot uses the French word *bizarre*, specifically in relationship to understanding of inherited biological differences between people and their appearance. He also uses the term more generally to describe many different typologies of *marginality*. Usually the term refers to a *bizarre* type that is capable of being *décousu*. In *Le Neveu de Rameau* a *bizarre* person is capable of finding truth because he is able to exist in the necessary state of unraveling, or *décousu*.

[259] Diderot, *Le Neveu*, 84.

to *tâtonnement* Diderot uses written expressions as his *enchaînements* and as a way of writing without inhibition. This type of expression also leads to a kind of intimacy with the reader. He confesses his preference to Sophie Volland when speaking of *Le Rêve de d'Alembert*: "Il n'est pas possible d'être plus profond et plus fou".[260] In this *folie* Diderot never forgets the importance of balancing out discovery and process. In this example from *Le Rêve de d'Alembert* we see the reference once again to process and presentation.

> BORDEU. Non; il a fait une assez belle excursion. Voilà de la philosophie bien haute ; systématique dans ce moment, je crois que plus les connaissances de l'homme feront des progrès, plus elle se vérifiera.[261]

The *excursion* to which Diderot refers is the *délire* in the unraveled state. In order to have a stroke of *genius*, one could be in a state of delirium. Diderot often refers to this state in *Le Rêve de d'Alembert* as the *délire philosophique*.

The experimental process requires *tâtonnement*, which is process of discovery by vibratory touching. Diderot speaks about the value of this process at length in the *Lettre sur les Aveugles*. It is simultaneously a mental and physical activity and sets up a symbiotic resonance between body and mind. This movement becomes a method of experimentation and is natural and instinctual in its application. The natural process according to Diderot's methodology is as it should be, and anything that is perfect represents the truth. *Tâtonnement,* as pointed out by Wilda Anderson in the following passage, is one pathway to finding truth.

> Only at this point, in spite of all the hints he had dropped, do we take seriously the idea that Diderot's unity of nature may be nonparadoxically antireductionist. Contemplation of the hypostatized unified nature suggests not minimalist natural laws, but "les essais les plus bizarres"; only the natural philosopher proves able to project and make comprehensible the

---

[260] Lettres of August 23, 1769 in: Denis Diderot, *Lettres à Sophie Volland*, ed. André Babélon (Paris: Gallimard, 1930), 204.

[261] Diderot, *Oeuvres Complètes*, 140.

results. To those without 'touch,' the experiments seem bizarre; to those who have not achieved the perception of nature's unity as complex, their results are astonishing.[262]

Here Anderson explains that *tâtonnement* is a method of experimentation that uses the power of *fantaisie*. *Tâtonnement* demands that the philosopher repeatedly re-establish contact with himself in order to avoid falling into the *"fureur des conjectures"* and produces a symbiotic relationship created between experimenter and nature.[263] This process engenders the kind of familiarity that is needed for real knowledge and truth. Even in his method of experimentation Diderot's emphasis is on process.

Perception and Truth

In *La lettre sur les Aveugles* Diderot repeats his "absence is presence" paradigm and uses sight to explain the experience of blindness. The mind-set of the *aveugle né* is examined in this work. Saunderson uses his memory and imagination in order to see. He sees geometry and arithmetic in figures. Other non-sighted people described in this piece also learned through their imagination and through the sensual world yet Diderot is intrigued by Saunderson:

> Je conviens encore qu'il est fait à l'imitation d'un autre qui n'est pas trop bon : mais je suis las d'en chercher un meilleur.[264]

With Saunderson, Diderot is linking sensual gaps to linguistic metaphors that will become central in *La lettre sur les sourds et muets*. To Diderot there were many sensory paths to the perception of truth. For example, the absence of one sense helps to emphasize others. As James Creech points out:

---

[262] Anderson, *Dream*, 21.

[263] The relationship between experimentation and nature is a main theme of the first half of the *Interprétation*.

[264] Diderot, *Lettres sur les aveugles*, 131.

In the *La Lettre sur les aveugles*, blindness is the metaphor for the representational space that both differentiates object and image and poses the very question of their identity or conformity.[265]

Creech explains that Diderot uses blindness as a metaphor in the same way as he uses insanity as a metaphor in *Le Neveu de Rameau*. The function of the metaphor of blindness is similar in its mirroring effect: it is used to reflect an image. In the *Lettre sur les Aveugles* Diderot moves from object to concept, thus helping to create a more concrete idea of the norm. Diderot announces this plainly when he comments about Saunderson: "Le nôtre parle de miroir à tout moment"[266]

Vanderheyden links the conjoined twins of *Le Rêve* to the blind character Saunderson in *Le Rêve de d'Alembert* by underscoring the idea of the mirror image. She discusses the manner in which Saunderson experiences the world as a projection of "being out of ourselves" of being able to relate to what is *other*:

> Understandably, the blind man's description of a mirror highlights the tactile and dense characteristics of the reflection of an object or of a body, similar to a statuesque reflection and also to the conjoined twins of Rabastens. Projecting us "out of ourselves," this multi-dimensional doubling is more effective than the one-dimensional mirror, and could thus represent the *modèle ideal* of mimesis that can never be achieved. As in the process of artistic mimesis, the deaf-mute and the *aveugle né* operate from a lack that can never be overcome no matter how hard he tries or how much one tries to describe certain objects to him, the blind man can never identify totally with these objects and concepts. Not unlike the spectator/interpreter of dreams, the blind man must draw analogies from the fragmented glimpses of meaning in order to ascertain or comprehend representation.[267]

The discussion of creativity in *La Lettre sur les aveugles* is connected to Diderot's many discussions of *geniu*s in his other works. The blind character Saunderson vacillates between instincts. He questions both process and

---

[265] Creech, *Thresholds*, 120.

[266] Diderot, *Lettres sur les aveugles*, 20.

[267] Jennifer Vanderheyden, *The Function of the Dream and the Body in Diderot's Works*, The Age of Revolution and Romanticism Interdisciplinary Studies, Vol. 31,(New York: Peter Lang, 2004), p.80.

presentation in the course of discovery. He uses not only a scientific methodology but also uses a creative manner of presentation. James Creech describes the expression of Saunderson in this way:

> The blindness of Saunderson produces neither the literal nor the figurative meaning of such language. It produces doubling in both the separation of the meanings and the coalescence of the trope.[268]

The above passage prefaces Diderot's use of paradox and metaphor as literary vehicles in his discussion of what is unraveled or *décousu*, as it explains his innovative tools and methods. Diderot construed a way to explain the meaning of Saunderson's methodology of abstract reasoning, to which he constantly refers in examples such as this one:

> Ces choses perdront beaucoup de leur merveilleux, si vous considérez, Madame, qu'il y a trois choses à distinguer dans toute question mêlée de physique et de géométrie ; le phénomène à expliquer, les suppositions du géomètre ; et le calcul qui résulte des suppositions. Or il est évident que, quelle que soit la pénétration d'un aveugle, les phénomènes de la lumière et des couleurs lui sont inconnus.[269]

In *La Lettre sur les aveugles* Saunderson "sees" things in a completely different way, and his creativity is ever present. To Diderot, Saunderson himself is a phenomenon that represents the *bizarre* and Saunderson's blindness provided Diderot with an opportunity to analyze the process of thought itself. Many other of the most relevant examples of Diderot's analysis of perceptual and mental processes are found in *Le Rêve de d'Alembert*, such as this discussion in which Bordeu proposes this definition of the working of the human mind:

---

[268] Creech, *Thresholds*, 115.

[269] Diderot, *Lettres sur les aveugles*, 42.

BORDEU. Et que c'est la mémoire et la comparaison qui s'ensuivent nécessairement de toutes ces impressions qui font la pensée et le raisonnement.[270]

Comparison of this passage from *Le Rêve de d'Alembert* to *La Lettre sur les aveugles* is instructive because we are reminded in the dialectical discussion between the characters of the important roles of memory and comparison. These are two faculties that Saunderson, the central figure in the *La Lettre sur les aveugles,* also possesses and that render him *bizarre.*

Word and Image

One cannot discuss Diderot's theories of perception and thought without mentioning his discussions of art. His writings on the *Salons* and his theories for the interpretation of visual aesthetics draw on what we have termed his vocabulary of marginalization and provide fertile ground for the expansion and completion of this study. The literary is supported by the visual and therefore the study of representation of the concept of in art would add another significant dimension to the study of *marginality* in the works of Diderot. Truth is easier to present in the world of the visual than in the realms of literature or science because, according to Diderot, the world of art and the imagination were not established in the world of fact. Therefore, in Diderot's *Salons* truth is openly presented through the vision of the artist.

The state of unraveling found in science especially in the form of experimentation is similar to the chaos of the creative process in art. Diderot's work presents organized chaos and explores the idea of the perfection in truth. Process is science and in this way is equal to the idea of chaos in artistic expression. Examples of non-linear process include Rameau's nephew in a state of *folie,* Suzanne Simonin in a state of hysteria, Saunderson, groping and blind, or

---

[270] Diderot, *Oeuvres Complètes*, 155.

d'Alembert in a feverish delirium. All are in a state that could be described as *décousu*.

Passion

The French word *passion* had multiple meanings in the eighteenth century. Many of these senses have continued to evolve into modern French usage. For Diderot, the idea of *passion* as stated earlier, is part and parcel of his idea of enthusiasm; indeed for him the notion of enthusiasm is an integral part of what makes passion. *Passion* and enthusiasm at very high levels, combined with intelligence and other important ingredients, are what make genius possible. Again in an article from the speculative arena of his *Pensées* Diderot explains what he means by *passion*. I note that in the *Eléments de physiologie* Diderot seems to be confused at times between raw emotion and passion. He describes *passion* most clearly in this way :

VII Passions
Il n'y a qu'une seule passion, celle d'être heureux. Elle prend différents noms suivants les objets. Elle est vice ou vertu selon sa violence, ses moyens et ses effets.[271]

If one follows Diderot's line of reasoning, women must be more capable of arriving at the truth than men because they are more likely to be found in a state of being "unraveled." Yet he never endows women with this capacity. Instead he states in *Sur les femmes* that women are held back intellectually by their passion.[272]

Because Diderot made the distinction between the ways the different sexes experience passion, some major questions arise. What of the large place given to passion in his works? If men and women are biologically different do they experience passion in the same way? If so, truths are not the same for both sexes.

---

[271] Denis Diderot, *Éléments de physiologie*, Jean M. Mayer, Oeuvres Complètes (Paris: Hermann, 1987), 486–7.

[272] Diderot, *Sur les femmes*. 41.

As Hill points out, recognizing the ambiguity of his position, Diderot felt obliged to defend it: "He coupled every argument in favor of the passions and the passionate man with a defense of his own morality."[273]

There seems to be another connection Diderot attempted to make here: the link between individual and society. The mothers superior act as mirrors to society as do the characters of the nephew and *Lui* in *Le Neveu de Rameau*. Diderot also makes clear this reciprocal relationship when he addresses the repression of the passions in his speculative works as found in these fragments from the *Pensées Philosophiques*:

Pensée V

C'est le comble de la folie que de se proposer la ruine des passions. Le beau projet que celui d'un dévot qui se tourmente comme un forcené pour ne rien désirer, ne rien aimer, ne rien sentir, et qui finirait par devenir un vrai monstre s'il réussissait.[274]

Pensée IV

Ce serait donc, un bonheur, me dira-t-on, d'avoir les passions fortes. Oui sans doute, si toutes sont à l'unisson. Etablissez entre elles une juste harmonie, et n'appréhendez point de désordres. Si l'espérance est balancée par la crainte, le point d'honneur par l'amour de la vie, le penchant au plaisir par l'intérêt de la santé, vous ne verrez ni libertins, ni téméraires, ni lâches.[275]

In the above sections in particular it seems that Diderot understood and emphasized what he saw to be the one true motivation of balanced passion: happiness. He further refines his view in *Les Eléments de physiologie*:

---

[273] Hill, "Monsters," 113.

[274] Denis Diderot, *Oeuvres philosophiques*, ed. Paul Vernière (Paris: Garnier, 1961), 11.

[275] Diderot, *Oeuvres philosophiques*, 11.

Les philosophes ne s'accordent pas sur le nombre des passions. Les passions de l'appétit concupisible font la volupté, et la douleur, la cupidité et la suite : l'amour et la haine.[276]

Blandine McLaughlin, in her article "Diderot and Women Notions," summarizes the concepts of passion and madness in Diderot's female characters:

Madness, an extreme form of passion is, for Diderot, the breaking of the link between the real and the mental. Imagination, like madness, of which it is a moderate form, is a distraction from reality, an indifference to its order.[277]

In the above passage, passion signals the process of unraveling, and again Diderot questions the extremes of behavior, especially in his quest for an understanding of genius. Passion is not only a danger to women; it can become especially dangerous in men as well. The overabundance of passion is a danger when not balanced with the right ingredients that constitute genius. It might lead to melancholia, or even madness which is what happened to Diderot's erstwhile friend Rousseau.[278]

As we have seen, Diderot tends to lump many concepts together in his works. Often the theme of melancholy is linked to passion and specifically to the suffering associated with it. The overriding presence of melancholy makes it a necessary part of the type of passion as we have seen presented in *La Religieuse*. It

---

[276] Diderot, *Éléments de physiologie*, 16.

[277] McLaughlin,"Diderot and Women". In many works of Diderot women are depicted as marginal, one reason being that they are prone to follow their emotions and not the law of reason. In *Sur les femmes* for example, Diderot points out that for women the uterus is the organ of thought, and that if this is the case then women are always governed by passion.

[278] Diderot, as we have seen in chapter three, also had a history of being overtaken by passion and melancholy. But according to Emita Hill, At times Diderot's melancholy was almost as profound as that of his friend Rousseau, the difference being that Diderot had learned how channel his feelings :

He cannot--like Rousseau, sever himself from other men when their behavior is too distasteful to him; he chooses rather to plunge deeper into the *Encyclopédie*, his appointed task that shall hasten the days of Enlightenment Hill, "Monsters," 147.

is also directly related to the French pre-romantic notion that those who suffer deep melancholy are often the greatest observers and artists; we see examples of this discussed throughout the work of Diderot, especially in *Le Neveu de Rameau*. There are those who are considered geniuses, and the typology is often juxtaposed against the backdrop of what Diderot considered to be mediocre. The genius, because of his extraordinary capabilities, was also outside the idea of the norm and therefore subject to Diderot's scrutiny.

Some further examples of Diderot's attempt to define genius show that he tried to describe it by identifying what it was not. For example, being gifted or talented is often confused with the idea of *génie*. Suzanne Simonin of *La Religieuse* does not possess genius but she has talent; this does not escape her notice when her audience responds enthusiastically even to her most modest efforts. We are constantly reminded that it is mere talent that is depicted here, it is not genius:

> Je ne sais ce que cela produisit, mais on ne m'écouta pas longtemps, on m'interrompit par des éloges que je fus bien surprise d'avoir mérités si promptement et à si peu de frais.[279]

Suzanne's ability was a vehicle for Diderot to discuss the origins and characteristics of genius. In the novel *La Religieuse* Suzanne's talent is more than just acceptable, because it is fused with her love of music. She has but to touch the keyboard and her talent and passion are evident. Her modesty even accentuates her talent. But we are always reminded it is mere talent that she possesses here; she does not display genius. [280]

---

[279] Diderot, *La Religieuse*, 115.

[280] In the *Réfutation suivie de l'ouvrage de l'homme d'Helvetius*, Diderot clearly states his disbelief that women could actually be geniuses: "Il dit: Les Sapho, les Hypathie, les Catherine furent les femmes de génie. Ajoutez: Et de ce petit nombre j'en concluerai une égale aptitude au génie dans l'un et dans l'autre sexe, et qu'une hirondelle fait le printemps" Diderot, *Réfutation*, 606. Diderot expresses in *Sur le femmes* that nature would not permit women a non-emotional type of personality. Emotion is not to be confused with enthusiasm. It is enthusiasm for Diderot that counts in the making of genius.

We also learn that passion alone is not genius. Diderot says that enthusiasm is an important part of *genius*, but he attests to the fact that it is much more complex than passion in the *Pensée* below:

Pensée XVI

Je me représente la vaste enceinte des sciences, comme un grand terrain parsemé de places obscures et de places éclairées. Nos travaux doivent avoir pour but, ou d'étendre les limites des places éclairées, ou de multiplier sur le terrain les centres des lumières. L'un appartient au génie qui crée ; l'autre à la sagacité qui perfectionne.[281]

Diderot tests the hypothesis that genius was innate, but in the fragment above, he acknowledge that actively cultivating one's own genius is also necessary. Nevertheless, even as nature is responsible for the genius and for his creativity, so to nurture is a key to understanding the concept of genius. As often found in Diderot's work, we see the mirror opposites of ideas. The dualistic tension creates contrasting principles which set up the dialectic style for which Diderot is known.

Diderot uses an array of creative and introspective approaches to determine and define the components of genius. In the case of Diderot's fiction, the act of reading becomes part of the discovery process. In many of Diderot's speculative and scientifically oriented works, such as *Les Eléments de physiologie* and the *Pensées sur l'interprétation de la nature*, the method of unraveling is used to good effect. In many of these works the themes of biological predeterminisim and creationism are juxtaposed against each other and active reasoning is used to engage the reader in a dialectical activity of discovery. The discovery process is conducted at first by unraveling the outer layers of an hypothesis. It is then accomplished by the technically minute attention to dialectical process. This effort

---

[281] Diderot, *Pensées*, 39.

undoubtedly functions to maintain the tension of Diderot's sense of chaotic order.[282]

Denis Diderot held an abiding interest in the nature of the marginalization of individuals and of certain groups of peoples which he demonstrated through the character depictions found in his novels, and also through the descriptions expounded in his philosophical works. Although he did not have the word "marginality" available as a tool, Diderot explored notions that related directly to nonconformity in various situations throughout his speculative and fictional works. He recognized that marginalization occurs for many different reasons and under many different guises, and that this process can occur among individuals or among groups of people, and he expressed his views through nuanced dialectical arguments that reflect his recognition that human behavior is multidimensional. In the dialectic format of Diderot's writing, we experience the ordinary and mediocre, extravagance, genius, passion and melancholy, all the requisite components for a complete encounter with *marginality*.

---

[282] This concept is discussed in detail by Lester Crocker in his book *Diderot's Chaotic Order*. (Princeton: Princeton University Press,) 1974.

Conclusion

Diderot, Truth and "*Le délire philosophique*"

Marginality is the key element in Diderot's search for truth, for it is this concept that serves as the common link between truth and genius. In Diderot's work, it is the genius who best represents the truth, and in Diderot's analysis typically the genius is marginalized. Thus, Diderot's preoccupation with genius is an extension of his search for truth. The genius becomes more clearly defined through Diderot's consideration of art, and the appreciation of artistic expression is for Diderot, yet another pathway to the discovery of truth. Thus Diderot's concepts of individuality, originality, and *marginality* are inextricably linked to the notion of genius and the search for truth.

As the marginal character of the genius held a special attraction for Diderot, in both *La Religieuse* and *Le Neveu de Rameau*, Diderot describes talent and in so doing, treats genius through the same process in a tension of juxtaposing extreme personality characteristics. Suzanne Simonin and her loveless relationship with her mother in *La Religieuse,* is but one example of Diderot's literary skill in positioning contrasting personality traits to demonstrate a point. In this particular instance he defines passion by revealing what it is not. The nephew in *Le Neveu de Rameau* is not a genius, and nature is largely responsible for his mediocrity. Both the philosopher and the nephew follow a dialogue of digressions which allow the reader to unravel and analyze truths that otherwise might never be examined. The nephew is bizarre as well as mediocre. He is a good musician, yet he is an even more talented *fou*. Once again the idea of genius is made clearer in this piece by process of exclusion. In *Le Rêve de d'Alembert*, the discourse is different, yet many of the messages are the same and this discourse of extremes inter alia also demonstrates the clearest examples of Diderot's ideas on materialism. The fragmentation of characters also serves as a method to showcase Diderot's new ideas on what components make up the notion of genius or *génie*. Genius is innate, but involves passion and requires a high level of enthusiasm. For Diderot it is the genius, while in the process of inspired unraveling who comes closest to truth. The dialectical process takes different forms according to each individual context. In Diderot's works, both speculative and fictional, it is evident that the word *bizarre* serves as the link between the marginalized genius and the pursuit of truth. Diderot exposes his most basic ideas on materialism by emotionally and psychically unraveling his characters in his fictional pieces.

Whereas many writers actually weave a story, carefully constructing a work word-by-word, Diderot takes the opposite tack. He presents ideas by deconstructing them. It is in the deconstructed state that we are able to fully comprehend the essence of his design. The *marginal* position that Diderot describes usually requires two things in the course of his quest for truth: the events, persons, or situations are always described as *bizarre* and the state they are in is always described as *décousu*. One key discovery of this study is that Diderot used the term *décousu* in every context where he employs the word *bizarre*. The notions *bizarre, décousu* and *marginality* therefore all serve Diderot's goal in his pursuit of truth. [283]

The concept of *marginality* in Diderot's works stems from many sources, and is expressed in varying ways and degrees. His interests in process and in materialist philosophy were apparent catalysts that catapulted Diderot towards evolving a modern concept of *marginality*. The language used in all three forms of marginality I have identified in this study, *self-imposed, forced*; and *biologically-predetermined*, is strikingly similar. Diderot's presentation of the concept of *marginality* is found both "unraveled" in the form of delirium and insane characters and in the more organized form in his speculative works.

Diderot's writing is a fertile ground for philosophical experimentation. One way to refer to his style is by the term he himself coined, "*délire philosophique*." A

---

[283] We have only to look at how many times the word décousu appears in Diderot's cha-racter descriptions in *La Religieuse* to underscore this point.

confession of the author regarding his own writing method presents itself in these first lines of *Les Pensées sur l'interprétation de la nature*:

> C'est de la nature que je vais écrire. Je laisserai les pensées se succéder sous ma plume, dans l'ordre même selon lequel les objets se sont offerts à ma réflexion, parce qu'elles n'en représenteront que mieux les mouvements et la marche de mon esprit.[284]

All of these forms of exploration allowed Diderot directly to address the question: "What is truth?" In fiction, Diderot's characters, while in the process of discovery, exemplify what it is to be in a state of *unraveling*. Diderot also believed that one could not arrive at the truth in science without following a defined series of steps. In the introduction to the *Eléments de physiologie* he said : "On ne peut pas deviner mais il faut suivre une série de conjectures."[285] The scientific method constituted another type of unraveling.

Diderot worked in diverse areas of written expression. In this study I have examined selected examples from his fiction, philosophy, science and art criticism. Each of these forms of writing exhibits a particular methodology, but the common goal is a quest for truth. Furthermore, in his pursuit of truth there is a distinct element of the quest that is described as a *process*. Two significant aspects of the *process* in the search for truth are: 1) it has patterns and 2) it evolves. Ernst Cassirer, in *The Philosophy of the Enlightenment*, equates the phenomenon of process in the search for truth with Diderot's view of the experimental process and emphasizes Diderot's insistence that the quest must be freed from all religious bonds: " . . . if the experimental process is to be completely effective, we must grant it full autonomy and free it from all tutelage"[286] The experimental process in each literary and speculative piece that Diderot wrote evolves and stands on its own.

---

[284] Diderot, *Pensées*, 27.

[285] Diderot, *Éléments de physiologie*, 462.

[286] Cassirer, *Enlightenment*, 74.

While Diderot's contribution to scientific and philosophical thought has received a good deal of recognition it is also important to note the centrality of his exploration of *marginality* to the body of his work.

Later in *Les Eléments de physiologie* Diderot further clarifies this idea : "l'expérience journalière des phénomènes forme la suite des idées, des sensations, des raisonnements, des sons".[287] In Diderot's fiction and in his speculative works scientific and philosophical truths he defined in tandem with the development of his ideas on materialism. Evidence for this is found in such speculative works as the *Eléments de Physiologie :* La chose devient plus aisée à concevoir, si j'ai la présence des objets.[288]

Diderot's view of the truth is not monistic; he recognizes that science needs details and facts for proof and art is not in the same rational realm as it requires a kind of introspective vehicle to produce truth. This awareness is also announced in the lines of the *Eléments de Physiologie*: On éprouve une sensation ; on a une idée ; on produit un son représentatif de cette sensation, ou commémoratif de cette idée.[289] Here Diderot highlights the idea that understanding scientific truth requires a rational state of being, whereas comprehending artistic and philosophical truth requires a distanced, less rational state for interpretation.

There is a level of chaos necessary for artistic discovery. Paradoxically, what is not absolute, (call it imperfection,) is part of absolute truth. As Herbert Dieckmann indicates Diderot recognizes the validity of the concept of poetic license:

> C'est là cependant la condition idéale de l'artiste, qui est en partie où à l'état virtuel le personnage de ses œuvres, qui peut s'identifier avec lui et

---

[287] Diderot, *Éléments de physiologie*, 464.

[288] Diderot, *Éléments de physiologie*, 462.

[289] Diderot, *Éléments de physiologie*, 463.

toutefois maintenir libres et disponibles son imagination et ses dons créateur.[290]

We have seen too how observation, reflection and experimentation were Diderot's analytical tools in the pursuit of knowledge.[291] Diderot well understood that experimentation was open-ended and the outcome was not necessarily what one intended. Therefore truth cannot be perfect. Action is part of truth. In science, experimental failures are intrinsic to the scientific process. Cassirer confirms this when discussing the *philosophes*:

> However perfect mathematics may be in its own province and to whatever precision it may evolve its concepts, yet this perfection will necessarily remain its imminent limitation. This reality becomes accessible to us only through experiment, through faithful and exact observations.[292]

Diderot derived his materialism by a denial of the mind-body opposition, by viewing the connections between mind and body as if they were one entity.[293] Diderot's *Salon of 1767* explores the failure of language to convey the mind's state of being. Art, for Diderot, is a tool and unifying force to express what language cannot. Process in science can in this way be compared with the idea of chaos in art. The experimental process need not be linear.

In conclusion I wish to stress that the popularization of the concept of *marginality* in our time has its roots in both Diderot's and Rousseau's eighteenth-century attempts to define the structure of the emerging nation-state and its social structures. I have sought to tease out Diderot's nascent concept of *marginality*, and to chronicle his fitful attempts to analyze and define it, in an

---

[290] Dieckmann, *Cinq*, 66.

[291] La méthode: Diderot, *Pensées*, XLI.

[292] Cassirer, *Enlightenment*, 74.

[293] The mind and body split was a popular concept in the seventeenth century. It was a concept derived from ancient Greek philosophy. This split is especially seen in the work of the precursors to the Enlightenment such as Descartes.

attempt to reveal the roots of some key modern psycho-social categorizations, especially in works such as *Le Neveu de Rameau*, Diderot's quintessential work on *marginality,* and in *La Religieuse*. Throughout, I have sought to illustrate that Diderot's writings are diverse and cannot be categorized into one genre; He wrote fiction, philosophical, and scientific treatises, as well as theatre and the art-historical and critical *Salons*, but whatever the genre, *marginality* comes to the fore. It is fundamental to our understanding of the modern concept of *marginality* to show how it functions within Diderot's fictional and speculative work and essential to recognize the importance of Diderot's contribution to modern thought and to an astonishing range of human endeavors.

Bibliography

Primary Sources

Diderot, Denis. *Encyclopédie*. First Edition, Facsimile. Ed. Jean Varloot. Œuvres Complètes. Cambridge MA: Houghton Library Rare Book Collection, 1812.
------. *Essais sur la peinture*. Ed. Gita M. May. Œuvres Complètes. Paris: Hermann, 1984.
------. *Éléments de physiologie*. Ed. Jean M. Mayer. Œuvres Complètes. Paris: Hermann, 1987.
------. *L'Entetien d'un père avec ses enfants*. Eds. Herbert Dieckmann and Jean Varloot. Œuvres Complètes. Paris: Hermann, 1989.
------. *Lettres à Sophie Volland*. Ed. André Babélon. Paris: Gallimard, 1930.
------. *Lettres sur les aveugles*. Ed. Robert Nicklaus. Œuvres Complètes. Paris: Hermann, 1978.
------. *Le Neveu de Rameau*. Ed. Herbert Dieckmann. Œuvres Complètes. Paris: Hermann, 1989.
------. *Œuvres Complètes*. In *Vol. XII, Supplément au Voyages de Bougainville*. Dieckmann, Herbert. Paris: Hermann, 1989.
------. *Œuvres Complètes*. Ed. H. Dieckmann. *Le Rêve de d'Alembert*. Paris: Hermann, 1975.
------. *Œuvres philosophiques*. Ed. Paul Vernière. Paris: Garnier, 1961.
------. *Pensées sur l'interprétation de la nature*. Ed. Jean Varloot. Œuvres Complètes. Paris: Hermann, 1978.
------. *La Religieuse*. Ed. Georges May. Œuvres Complètes. Paris: Hermann, 1975.
------. *La Réfutation suivie de l'ouvrage d'Helvétius intitulé l'Homme*. Ed. Paul Vernière. Œuvres philosophiques. Paris: Garnier, 1961.
------. *Sur les femmes*. Ed. Elizabeth Badinter. Paris: Plon, 1989.
------. *Textes choisis de l'Encyclopédie*. Ed. Albert Soboul. Œuvres Complètes. Paris: Editions Sociales, 1952.

Secondary Sources

Aarslef, Hans. "The Tradition of Condillac: The Origin of Language in the Eighteenth Century and the Debate in the Berlin Academy." *From Locke to Saussure: Essays on the Study of Language and Intellectual History.* Minneapolis: University of Minnesota Press, 1982, 147-160.

Anderson, Wilda. *Diderot's Dream.* Baltimore: Johns Hopkins University Press, 1990.

Arden, Heather. *Fools Plays: A Study of Satire in the Sottie.* London: Cambridge University Press, 1980.

Aries, Philippe. *Centuries of Childhood.* New York: Vintage Random House, 1962.

Benrekassa, Georges. *Le Concentrique et L'Excentrique: Marges Des Lumières.* Paris: Payot, 1980.

Berlin, Isaiah. *Karl Marx.* London: Oxford University Press, 1948.

Brecht, Berthold. "A Short Organum for the Theatre." *Avant Garde Drama*, Ed. Bernard Dukore and Daniel C. Gerould, New York: Bantam, 1969.

Caplan, Jay. *Framed Narratives: Diderot's Genealogy of The Beholder.* Minneapolis: Minnesota University Press, 1985.

Cassirer, Ernst. *The Philosophy of the Enlightenment.* Princeton: Princeton University Press, 1960.

Creech, James. *Diderot: Thresholds of Representation.* Columbus: Ohio University Press, 1986.

Crocker, Lester. *Diderot's Chaotic Order.* Princeton: Princeton University Press, 1974.

Damrosch, Leo. *Jean-Jacques Rousseau: Restless Genius.* Boston: Houghton Mifflin, 2005.

Dictionnaire de Trévoux. Paris: Libraires Associés, 1752.

Dieckmann, Herbert. *Cinq Leçons sur Diderot.* Genève: Librairie Droz, 1959.

------. "Diderot's Conception of Genius." *Journal of the History of Ideas* 2:2 (April 1941), 151–82.

Duncan, Carol. "Happy Mothers and Other New Ideas in French Art." *The Art Bulletin* 55:4, (December 1973), 570–83.

Fellows, Otis. "The Theme of Genius in Diderot's *Neveu de Rameau*," *Diderot Studies* II (1952) : 168–99.

Foucault, Michel. *Histoire de la Folie à l'âge classique.* Paris: Gallimard, 1972.

_____. *Les mots et les choses: une archéologie des sciences humaines.* Paris: Gallimard, 1966.

Gilman, Sander. "Psychiatry and Psychoanalysis." *Critical Inquiry* 13:2 (Winter 1987), 293–313.

Harrap's French Dictionary.

Hill, Emita. "The Theme of Monsters in the Works of Denis Diderot." Cambridge: Harvard University Press, 1972.

Kant, Immanuel. *Critique of Pure Reason*. Trans. Norman Kemp Smith. New York: St Martin's Press, 1965)

Kristeva, Julia. *Desire in Language*. Trans. Leon Rowdies. New York: Columbia University Press, 1980.

------. *Etrangers à Nous-Mêmes*. Paris: Gallimard, 1988.

Laplanche, Jean, and J-B. Pontalis. *The Language of Psycho-Analysis*. New York: Norton, 1973.

------. *Vocabulaire de la Psychoanalyse*. Paris: Presses Universitaires Françaises, 1967.

Mandel, Ernst, and George Novack. *The Marxist Theory of Alienation*. New York: Pathfinder, 1974.

Mauzi, Robert. "Préface." In *La Religieuse*, Denis Diderot, 9–42. Paris: Gallimard, 1974.

May, Georges. "Diderot et La Religieuse." New Haven: Yale University Press, 1954.

May, Gita. "Diderot and Burke: A Study in Aesthetic Affinity." *PMLA* 75 (December 1960), 527–39.

------. "Rousseau's Anti-Feminism Reconsidered." In *French Women and the Age of Enlightenment*, Ed. Samia Spencer, 309–17. Bloomington: Indiana University Press, 1984.

McDonald, Christie. *The Dialogue of Writing*. Waterloo, Ontario: Wilfred Laurier University Press, 1984.

McLaughlin, Blandine. "Diderot and Women." In *French Women and the Age of Enlightenment*, Ed. Samia Spencer, 296–308. Bloomington: Indiana University Press, 1984.

Mehlman, Jeffrey. *Cataract: A Study in Diderot*. Middletown, CT: Wesleyan University Press, 1979.

Mortier, Roland, and Raymond Trousson, Eds. *Dictionnaire de Diderot*. Paris: Honoré Champion, 1999.

The Oxford English Dictionary.

Parke, Robert. "Human Migration and the *Marginal* Man." *The American Journal of Sociology* 6 (May 1928), 881–93.

Proust, Jacques. *Diderot et L'Encyclopédie*. Paris: Armand Colin, 1967.

Pucci, Suzanne. *Diderot and a Poetics of Science*. New York: Peter Lang, 1986.

Robert, Paul. *Dictionnaire alphabétique et analogique de la langue française*. Paris: Le Robert, 1985.

Roy, Maria. *Battered Women: A Psychosociological Study of Domestic Violence*. New York: Van Nostrand Reinhold, 1977.

Schama, Simon. *Citizens; A Chronicle of the French Revolution*. New York: Knopf, 1989.

Serres, Michel. *Le Parasite*. Paris: Grasset, 1980.

Simon, Bennett. *Mind and Madness in Ancient Greece: The Classical Roots of the Modern*. New York: Cornell University Press, 1978.

Simon, Julia. *Mass Enlightenment:* Critical Studies: Rousseau and Diderot. New York: SUNY Press. 1995.

Stockinger, Jacob. "Homosexuality in the French Enlightenment." In *Homosexualities and French Literature*, Ed. Elaine Marks, 167–9. Ithaca, NY: Cornell University Press, 1979.

Todorov, Tzvetan. *La Conquête de l'Amérique*. Paris: Seuil, 1982.

------. *Nous et les Autres*. Paris: Seuil, 1989.

Trilling, Lionel. *Prefaces to the Experience of Literature*. New York: Harcourt Brace Jovanovich, 1981.

------. *Sincerity and Authenticity*. Cambridge: Harvard University Press, 1972.

Vanderheyden, Jennifer. *The Function of the Dream and the Body in Diderot's Works*, The Age of Revolution and Romanticism: Interdisciplinary Studies 31. New York: Peter Lang, 2004.

Vartanian, Aram. "The Preamble to Diderot's *Pensées sur l'Interprétation de la Nature*: A Decoding." *Romantic Review*, January 1985, 24–35.

Wilson, Arthur McCandless. *Diderot: The Testing Years*. New York: Oxford University Press, 1957.

Index

Barbara Lise Abrams

Dr. Barbara L. Abrams is an Associate Professor of French and Humanities at Suffolk University in Boston, Massachusetts. Dr. Abrams completed her Ph.D. in French Literature at Columbia University in New York.